MW01256054

2024

SOCCER LEGENDS

Printed and bound in Dubai
Author: David Ballheimer
Senior Commissioning Editor: Suhel Ahmed
Design Manager: Matt Drew
Picture research: Paul Langan
Production: Arlene Alexander

All facts and stats correct as of June 2023

PICTURE CREDITS
The publishers would like to thank the following sources for their kind permission to reproduce the pictures in this book.

GETTY IMAGES: Aitor Alcalde 61; Ion Alcoba/Quality Sport Images 57; Filippo Alfero/Juventus FC 102; Eric Alonso 27; Emilio Andreoli 11, 83, 103, 107T; Gonzalo Arroyo Moreno 48, 76; Matthew Ashton/AMA 47; Marc Atkins 80; Sam Bagnall/AMA 28; Robbie Jay Barratt/AMA 55, 99, 109T; Giuseppe Bellini 17; Berengui/DeFodi Images 8; John Berry 21, 74, 90; Romain Biard/Icon Sport 106B; Shaun Botterill 44; Paolo Bruno 49; Clive Brunskill 13; David S. Bustamante/Soccrates 22, 60, 65; Pedro Castillo/Real Madrid 34; Jean Catuffe 16, 54; James Chance 94; Matteo Ciambelli/NurPhoto 67; Emmanuele Ciancaglini/Ciancaphoto Studio 69; Gareth Copley 106T; Oscar Del Pozo/AFP 111B; Paul Ellis/AFP 85; Julian Finney 38; Stuart Franklin 92; Alex Gottschalk/DeFodi Images 33; Laurence Griffiths 40; Matthias Hangst 73, 77; Alexander Hassenstein 97; Mike Hewitt 59; Mario Hommes/DeFodi Images 51, 79; Catherine Ivill 12; Chloe Knott/Danehouse 43; Roland Krivec/DeFodi Images 30; Maurizio Lagana 111T; Chris Lee/Chelsea FC 82; Sylvain Lefevre 24; Alex Livesey/Danehouse 39, 68, 91; Marco Luzzani 64, 72; Stuart MacFarlane/Arsenal FC 53; Giuseppe Maffia/NurPhoto 56; Manchester City FC 108B; Angel Martinez 26, 62; Matt McNulty/Manchester City FC 20, 35, 66; Aurelien Meunier/PSG 75; Alex Morton 89; Jonathan Moscrop 29; Alex Pantling 41; Ulrik Pedersen/DeFodi Images 15; Valerio Pennicino 108T; Andrew Powell/Liverpool FC 25; Pressinphoto/Icon Sport 45; Quality Sport Images 88; David Ramos 96; Michael Regan 78, 86, 107B; Alessandro Sabattini 93; Christophe Saidi/FEP/Icon Sport 105; Pedro Salado/Quality Sport Images 14; Fran Santiago 71, 87; Oli Scarff/AFP 5; Justin Setterfield 63, 95, 110T; Alexandre Simoes/Borussia Dortmund 18, 37; Diego Souto/Quality Sport Images 50, 98; Christof Stache/AFP 23; Simon Stacpoole/Offside 101; Jack Thomas/WWFC 7; Tottenham Hotspur FC 70; VI Images 81; Mateo Villalba/Quality Sport Images 36, 109B; Visionhaus 9, 19, 31, 42, 46, 52; Darren Walsh/Chelsea FC 10, 110B; George Wood 100

Every effort has been made to acknowledge correctly and contact the source and/or copyright holder of each picture any unintentional errors or omissions will be corrected in future editions of this book.

2024

SOCCER LEGENDS

STATS • PROFILES • TOP PLAYERS

MORTIMER

CONTENTS

HOW TO USE THIS BOOK

Welcome to *Soccer Legends 2024*—the exciting book packed with the performance stats of today's biggest stars in the world of soccer! We have chosen more than 100 players and managers from the world's top five leagues: The Bundesliga in Germany, La Liga in Spain, France's Ligue 1, the Italian Serie A, and the English Premier League. **The players are either playing in these leagues or have spent the prime years of their careers up until the 22/23 season operating in these top leagues.**

You can use this book to work out who you think are the best performers or even to get together with friends and play a kind of game of trading cards, comparing the performance records of today's finest defenders, midfielders, forwards, goalkeepers, and managers.

The types of stats featured for each position vary, because each position performs a specific role on the field. For example, a defender's main job is to stop the opposition from scoring, so the stats focus mainly on this part of that player's game. Likewise, a striker's tackling is not as relevant as the player's goal or assists tally. What you will find for all the players is the heat map, which shows how much of the field a player covers and which areas he focuses his play in or, with goalkeepers, whether their strengths lie in the six-yard box or playing as sweeper keepers, who are comfortable all around the penalty area.

The stats span a player's career to date, playing for teams belonging to one of the top five European leagues. The figures have been collected from only domestic league and European match appearances and exclude data from domestic cup, super cups, or international games. This narrow data pool means that the information is instantly comparable, so you can decide for yourself who truly deserves to be known as a living legend of the beautiful game.

DEFENDERS

There are different types of defenders. They cover a range of positions and have different skills. The centerbacks are the big defenders in the middle who mark the opposition strikers. Fullbacks operate out wide: They are quick, agile, and try to stop wide attackers from crossing balls into the box. Wingers play out wide, too, in front of the centerbacks, but they also make attacking runs when they have the chance. Finally, the sweeper is the spare defender who is positioned behind the centerback, ready to help the back four deal with any danger.

WHAT DO THESE STATS MEAN?

75%

AERIAL DUELS WON
This is the percentage of headers a defender has won in his own penalty area to interrupt an opposition attack.

INTERCEPTIONS
This is the number of times a defender has successfully stopped an attack without needing to make a tackle.

BLOCKS
A shot that is intercepted by a defender—preventing his keeper from having to make a save—counts as a block.

KEY PASSES/PASS COMPLETION
A key pass is one that results in an attacking opportunity. Pass completion indicates, as a percentage, the player's passing accuracy.

CLEARANCES
An attack successfully foiled, either by kicking or heading the ball away from danger, is regarded as a clearance.

TACKLES
This is the number of times a defender has challenged and dispossessed the opposition without committing a foul.

Did you know?

For about 40 years, from the late nineteenth century, the most common formation was 2–3–5. It featured only two defenders (right back and left back), while the centerback played in midfield. There were five forwards.

NATIONALITY
Austrian

CURRENT CLUB
Real Madrid

4

DAVID ALABA

Although his best position is left back, David Alaba's strength is his versatility. Superb with his positioning and reading of the game, his pace and athleticism also allow him to snuff out attacks before they have begun.

DATE OF BIRTH	06/24/1992
POSITION	LEFT BACK
HEIGHT	5 FT. 10¾ IN.
WEIGHT	172 LB.
PREFERRED FOOT	LEFT

BLOCKS 129

APPEARANCES 465

INTERCEPTIONS 580

AERIAL DUELS WON 49%

PASS COMPLETION 89%

PENALTIES SCORED 3

GOALS 33

KEY PASSES 405

CLEARANCES 632

TACKLES 572

MAJOR CLUB HONORS
⚽ La Liga: 2022, runner-up 2023 ⚽ Bund'liga: 2010, 2013-21 (x9 all B. Mun.) ⚽ UEFA Champs L.: 2013, 2020 (all B. Mun.), 2022 ⚽ FIFA Club World Cup: 2013, 2020 (all B. Mun.), 2022 ⚽ UEFA Super Cup: 2022 ⚽ Copa del Rey: 2023

INTERNATIONAL HONORS
⚽ None to date

ACTIVITY AREAS

TRENT ALEXANDER-ARNOLD

Counted among the world's best overlapping defenders, Trent Alexander-Arnold plays at right back or right winger. He is fast, tackles superbly, and is capable of whipping in accurate crosses that strikers love to feast on!

NATIONALITY
English

CURRENT CLUB
Liverpool

66

DATE OF BIRTH	10/07/1998
POSITION	FULLBACK
HEIGHT	5 FT. 9 IN.
WEIGHT	159 LB.
PREFERRED FOOT	RIGHT

APPEARANCES
250

BLOCKS
34

INTERCEPTIONS
318

AERIAL DUELS WON
37%

PENALTIES SCORED
0

PASS COMPLETION
78%

GOALS
14

KEY PASSES
497

CLEARANCES
361

TACKLES
418

MAJOR CLUB HONORS
⚽ Premier League: 2020 ⚽ UEFA Champions League: 2019
⚽ UEFA Champions League: Runner-up 2018, runner-up 2022
⚽ FIFA Club World Cup: 2019 ⚽ FA Cup 2022

INTERNATIONAL HONORS
⚽ UEFA Nations League: Third place 2019

ACTIVITY AREAS

28

NATIONALITY
Spanish

CURRENT CLUB
Chelsea

CÉSAR AZPILICUETA

Right back César Azpilicueta is a natural leader who can play anywhere on the field. He is excellent at using his positional sense to snuff out danger and frequently starts counterattacks with a great right foot.

DATE OF BIRTH	08/28/1989
POSITION	FULLBACK
HEIGHT	5 FT. 10 IN.
WEIGHT	168 LB.
PREFERRED FOOT	RIGHT

APPEARANCES
588

BLOCKS
201

INTERCEPTIONS
1,077

AERIAL DUELS WON
58%

PENALTIES SCORED
0

PASS COMPLETION
82%

GOALS
15

KEY PASSES
408

TACKLES
1,543

CLEARANCES
1,823

MAJOR CLUB HONORS
⚽ Premier League: 2015, 2017 ⚽ UEFA Champions League: 2021 ⚽ UEFA Europa League: 2013, 2019
⚽ FIFA Club World Cup: 2021, runner-up 2012 ⚽ UEFA Super Cup: 2021 ⚽ FA Cup: 2018, 2021, runner-up 2022

INTERNATIONAL HONORS
⚽ UEFA Nations League: Runner-up 2021
⚽ FIFA Confederations Cup: Runner-up 2013

ACTIVITY AREAS

LEONARDO BONUCCI

Italy's captain since 2022, Leonardo Bonucci is a strong and experienced centerback with exceptional ball skills. He is superb at breaking up play and launching attacks with long passes. What's more, he poses a goal threat from set pieces.

NATIONALITY
Italian

CURRENT CLUB
Juventus

19

DATE OF BIRTH	05/01/1987
POSITION	CENTER
HEIGHT	6 FT. 2¾ IN.
WEIGHT	187 LB.
PREFERRED FOOT	RIGHT

APPEARANCES
538

INTERCEPTIONS
887

BLOCKS
337

AERIAL DUELS WON
54%

PASS COMPLETION
87%

GOALS
34

PENALTIES SCORED
3

KEY PASSES
157

CLEARANCES
2177

TACKLES
608

MAJOR CLUB HONORS
- Serie A: 2006 (Inter Milan), 2012, 2013, 2014, 2015, 2016, 2017, 2019, 2020
- Coppa Italia: 2015, 2016, 2017, 2021

INTERNATIONAL HONORS
- UEFA European Championship: 2020-runner-up 2012
- FIFA Confederations Cup: Third place 2013
- UEFA Nations League: Third place 2021, third place 2023

ACTIVITY AREAS

3

NATIONALITY
Portuguese

CURRENT CLUB
Manchester City

RÚBEN DIAS

Rúben Dias plays mainly on the left side of center defense, but he is comfortable anywhere along the back line. He excels at winning challenges in the air and on the ground, making interceptions and delivering great passes with both feet.

DATE OF BIRTH	05/14/1997
POSITION	CENTER
HEIGHT	6 FT. 1¼ IN.
WEIGHT	168 LB.
PREFERRED FOOT	RIGHT

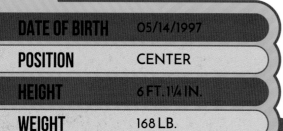

BLOCKS
79

APPEARANCES
139

INTERCEPTIONS
126

AERIAL DUELS WON
58%

PASS COMPLETION
92%

PENALTIES SCORED
0

GOALS
6

KEY PASSES
33

CLEARANCES
365

TACKLES
158

MAJOR CLUB HONORS
⚽ Premier League: 2021, 2022, 2023 ⚽ UEFA Champions League: Runner-up 2021, 2023 ⚽ Portuguese Premier Liga: 2019 (Benfica) ⚽ FA Cup: 2023

INTERNATIONAL HONORS
⚽ UEFA Nations League: 2019

ACTIVITY AREAS

VIRGIL VAN DIJK

Virgil van Dijk has returned to the form he showed before his 2020 knee injury. Good with either foot, he is a great tackler, a superb leader, wins headers in both penalty boxes, and reads the game excellently.

NATIONALITY
Dutch

CURRENT CLUB
Liverpool

DATE OF BIRTH	06/20/1991
POSITION	CENTER
HEIGHT	6 FT. 4¾ IN.
WEIGHT	203 LB.
PREFERRED FOOT	RIGHT

APPEARANCES
291

BLOCKS
139

INTERCEPTIONS
449

AERIAL DUELS WON
74%

PENALTIES SCORED
0

PASS COMPLETION
88%

GOALS
24

KEY PASSES
71

CLEARANCES
1,481

TACKLES
281

MAJOR CLUB HONORS
⚽ Premier League: 2020 ⚽ Scottish Premiership: 2014, 2015 (Celtic) ⚽ UEFA Champions League: 2019, runner-up 2018, runner-up 2022 ⚽ FIFA Club World Cup: 2019 ⚽ FA Cup: 2022

INTERNATIONAL HONORS
⚽ UEFA Nations League: Runner-up 2019

ACTIVITY AREAS

2

NATIONALITY
Uruguayan

CURRENT CLUB
Atlético Madrid

JOSÉ GIMÉNEZ

The Uruguayan is a tough tackling centerback who is quick off the mark and difficult to knock off the ball. He made his international debut when he was just 19 and has also thrived at club level since joining Atlético Madrid in 2013.

DATE OF BIRTH	01/20/1995
POSITION	CENTER
HEIGHT	6 FT. ¾ IN.
WEIGHT	170 LB.
PREFERRED FOOT	RIGHT

APPEARANCES
258

BLOCKS
154

INTERCEPTIONS
423

AERIAL DUELS WON
66%

PASS COMPLETION
83%

PENALTIES SCORED
0

GOALS
9

KEY PASSES
51

CLEARANCES
1,163

TACKLES
390

MAJOR CLUB HONORS
⚽ La Liga: 2014, 2021
⚽ UEFA Europa League: 2018
⚽ UEFA Super Cup: 2018
⚽ UEFA Champions League: Runner-up 2014, 2016

INTERNATIONAL HONORS
⚽ FIFA U-20 World Cup: Runner-up 2013
⚽ China Cup: 2018, 2019

ACTIVITY AREAS

JOŠKO GVARDIOL

The 21-year-old Joško Gvardiol has emerged as one of the bright lights in the Bundesliga. His abilities to defend in one-to-one situations, play the ball out of the back, and pick out the right pass make him a model modern-day centerback.

NATIONALITY
Croatian

CURRENT CLUB
RB Leipzig

32

DATE OF BIRTH	01/23/2002
POSITION	CENTER
HEIGHT	6 FT. ¾ IN.
WEIGHT	176 LB.
PREFERRED FOOT	LEFT

APPEARANCES
87

BLOCKS
38

INTERCEPTIONS
126

PENALTIES SCORED
0

AERIAL DUELS WON
58%

PASS COMPLETION
86%

GOALS
6

KEY PASSES
35

CLEARANCES
192

TACKLES
110

MAJOR CLUB HONORS
⚽ DFB Pokal: 2022, 2023

INTERNATIONAL HONORS
⚽ FIFA World Cup: Third place 2022

ACTIVITY AREAS

15

2

NATIONALITY
Moroccan

CURRENT CLUB
Paris Saint-Germain

ACHRAF HAKIMI

Born in Spain to Moroccan parents, Ashraf Hakimi has played and enjoyed success at some of Europe's top clubs. Known for his blistering pace and smart attacking instincts, he can play as a midfielder or winger, and he can even score and create goals.

DATE OF BIRTH	11/04/1998
POSITION	RIGHT BACK
HEIGHT	5 FT. 11¼ IN.
WEIGHT	161 LB.
PREFERRED FOOT	RIGHT

APPEARANCES
196

BLOCKS
20

INTERCEPTIONS
167

AERIAL
DUELS WON
42%

PENALTIES
SCORED
0

PASS COMPLETION
87%

GOALS
29

KEY PASSES
186

CLEARANCES
157

TACKLES
361

MAJOR CLUB HONORS
- ⚽ Ligue 1: 2022, 2023
- ⚽ Serie A: 2021 (Inter Milan)
- ⚽ UEFA Champions League: 2018 (R. Madrid)
- ⚽ FIFA World Club Cup: 2017 (R. Madrid)

INTERNATIONAL HONORS
- ⚽ None to date

ACTIVITY AREAS

THEO HERNÁNDEZ

Known more for his attacking qualities than his defensive work, Theo Hernández (younger brother of Lucas) is a soccer player who is blessed with great pace, can dribble rapidly with the ball at his feet, and possesses the capability to get into goal-scoring positions. He has become a fan favorite at AC Milan.

NATIONALITY
French

CURRENT CLUB
AC Milan

19

DATE OF BIRTH	10/06/1997
POSITION	LEFT BACK
HEIGHT	6 FT. ½ IN.
WEIGHT	179 LB.
PREFERRED FOOT	LEFT

BLOCKS
45

APPEARANCES
225

INTERCEPTIONS
231

PENALTIES SCORED
3

AERIAL DUELS WON
64%

PASS COMPLETION
83%

GOALS
25

KEY PASSES
246

CLEARANCES
297

TACKLES
384

MAJOR CLUB HONORS
⚽ Serie A: 2022 ⚽ UEFA Champions League 2017 (R. Madrid) ⚽ FIFA World Club Cup: 2017 (R. Madrid) ⚽ UEFA Super Cup 2017 (R. Madrid)

INTERNATIONAL HONORS
⚽ FIFA World Cup: Runner-up 2022 ⚽ UEFA Nations League: 2021

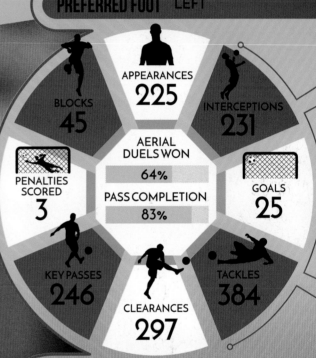

ACTIVITY AREAS

15

NATIONALITY
German

CURRENT CLUB
Borussia Dortmund

MATS HUMMELS

The German is regarded as one of the best ball-playing defenders on the planet. Hummels can physically tussle with the strongest of forwards, but it is his ability to stride forward and set up attacks with his fine passing that sets him apart.

DATE OF BIRTH	12/16/1988
POSITION	CENTER
HEIGHT	6 FT. 3 IN.
WEIGHT	207 LB.
PREFERRED FOOT	RIGHT

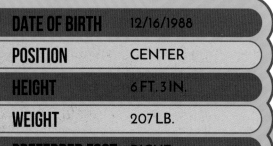

BLOCKS
231

APPEARANCES
513

INTERCEPTIONS
1,114

AERIAL DUELS WON
67%

PENALTIES SCORED
1

PASS COMPLETION
84%

GOALS
36

KEY PASSES
188

CLEARANCES
2,091

TACKLES
1,188

MAJOR CLUB HONORS
⚽ Bundesliga: 2011, 2012, 2017 (B. Mun), 2018 (B. Munich), 2019 (B. Munich), runner-up 2023 ⚽ DFB-Pokal: 2012, 2019 (B. Mun), 2021 ⚽ UEFA Champions League: Runner-up 2013

INTERNATIONAL HONORS
⚽ FIFA World Cup: 2014

ACTIVITY AREAS

KALIDOU KOULIBALY

Kalidou Koulibaly is an aggressive centerback, perfect for his side's high-pressing game. Extremely fast, he is capable of sprinting back to cover even if the opposition play the ball over the top or in behind his team's high defensive line.

NATIONALITY
Senegalese

CURRENT CLUB
Chelsea

26

DATE OF BIRTH	06/20/1991
POSITION	CENTER
HEIGHT	6 FT. 1¼ IN.
WEIGHT	196 LB.
PREFERRED FOOT	RIGHT

APPEARANCES
340

INTERCEPTIONS
557

BLOCKS
271

AERIAL DUELS WON
56%

PASS COMPLETION
88%

PENALTIES SCORED
0

GOALS
15

KEY PASSES
95

CLEARANCES
1,204

TACKLES
662

MAJOR CLUB HONORS
⚽ Belgian Cup: 2013 (Genk)
⚽ Coppa Italia: 2020 (Napoli)

INTERNATIONAL HONORS
⚽ Africa Cup of Nations: 2021, runner-up 2019

ACTIVITY AREAS

19

NATIONALITY
Spanish

CURRENT CLUB
Manchester City

AYMERIC LAPORTE

Aymeric Laporte has become one of Europe's best center defenders. Very strong, he is powerful in the tackle, excellent in the air, and a good organizer at the back. Laporte can also start attacks with his precise passing out of defense.

DATE OF BIRTH	05/27/1994
POSITION	CENTER
HEIGHT	6 FT. 2¼ IN.
WEIGHT	189 LB.
PREFERRED FOOT	LEFT

APPEARANCES
344

INTERCEPTIONS
635

BLOCKS
135

AERIAL DUELS WON
65%

PASS COMPLETION
88%

PENALTIES SCORED
0

GOALS
17

KEY PASSES
85

TACKLES
559

CLEARANCES
1,213

MAJOR CLUB HONORS
⚽ Premier League: 2018, 2019, 2021, 2022, 2023
⚽ UEFA Champions League: Runner-up 2021, 2023
⚽ FA Cup: 2019, 2023

INTERNATIONAL HONORS
⚽ UEFA Nations League: Runner-up 2021, 2023
⚽ UEFA European U-19 Championship: Runner-up 2013 (France)

ACTIVITY AREAS

MARQUINHOS

Marquinhos is a smart defender. He may not be a powerhouse like many of today's top-class centerbacks, but has the speed, agility, and intelligence to mark the quickest forwards, plus he can be very effective going forward.

NATIONALITY
Brazilian

CURRENT CLUB
Paris Saint-Germain

5

DATE OF BIRTH	05/14/1994
POSITION	CENTER
HEIGHT	6 FT.
WEIGHT	165 LB.
PREFERRED FOOT	RIGHT

APPEARANCES
376

BLOCKS
231

INTERCEPTIONS
502

AERIAL DUELS WON
58%

PASS COMPLETION
93%

PENALTIES SCORED
0

GOALS
33

KEY PASSES
76

CLEARANCES
1,299

TACKLES
574

MAJOR CLUB HONORS
⚽ Ligue 1: 2014, 2015, 2016, 2018, 2019, 2020, 2022, 2023 ⚽ UEFA Champions League: Runner-up 2020 ⚽ Coupe de France: 2015, 2016, 2017, 2018, 2020, 2021

INTERNATIONAL HONORS
⚽ Copa América: 2019, runner-up 2021
⚽ Olympic Games: 2016

ACTIVITY AREAS

16

NATIONALITY
Argentinian

CURRENT CLUB
Atlético Madrid

NAHUEL MOLINA

Nahuel Molina has worked hard to become a dominant force on the right flank. Very quick, with fine positional sense and good tackling technique, he is also comfortable with the ball at his feet and a tremendous passer in attacking situations.

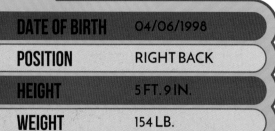

DATE OF BIRTH	04/06/1998
POSITION	RIGHT BACK
HEIGHT	5 FT. 9 IN.
WEIGHT	154 LB.
PREFERRED FOOT	RIGHT

BLOCKS
15

APPEARANCES
103

INTERCEPTIONS
62

AERIAL DUELS WON
39%

PASS COMPLETION
78%

PENALTIES SCORED
0

GOALS
13

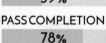

KEY PASSES
106

CLEARANCES
122

TACKLES
143

MAJOR CLUB HONORS
⚽ None to date

INTERNATIONAL HONORS
⚽ FIFA World Cup: 2022
⚽ Copa América: 2021

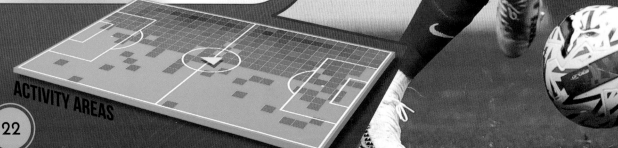

ACTIVITY AREAS

BENJAMIN PAVARD

Benjamin Pavard has matured into a technically brilliant defender. He has the ability to time his tackle perfectly and shut down opposing players in possession of the ball. He can also move the ball down one or two lines of defense with a single pass.

NATIONALITY
French

CURRENT CLUB
Bayern Munich

5

DATE OF BIRTH	03/28/1996
POSITION	CENTER
HEIGHT	6 FT. 1¼ IN.
WEIGHT	168 LB.
PREFERRED FOOT	RIGHT

APPEARANCES
229

BLOCKS
112

INTERCEPTIONS
396

PENALTIES SCORED
0

AERIAL DUELS WON
61%

PASS COMPLETION
87%

GOALS
11

KEY PASSES
110

CLEARANCES
688

TACKLES
332

MAJOR CLUB HONORS
⚽ Bundesliga: 2020, 2021, 2022, 2023 ⚽
UEFA Champions League: 2020 ⚽ UEFA Super Cup: 2020
⚽ FIFA Club World Cup: 2020 ⚽ DFB-Pokal: 2020

INTERNATIONAL HONORS
⚽ FIFA World Cup: 2018, runner-up 2022
⚽ UEFA Nations League: 2021

ACTIVITY AREAS

23

4*

*At Paris Saint-Germain

NATIONALITY
Spanish

CURRENT CLUB
TBC

SERGIO RAMOS

Very quick at anticipating danger, Sergio Ramos is a fine tackler with an excellent positional sense. Not only is he a skilled defender and great team leader, but is also known for regularly scoring important goals for his team.

DATE OF BIRTH	03/30/1986
POSITION	CENTER
HEIGHT	6 FT. ½ IN.
WEIGHT	181 LB.
PREFERRED FOOT	RIGHT

APPEARANCES
696

BLOCKS
319

INTERCEPTIONS
1,482

AERIAL DUELS WON
67%

PASS COMPLETION
88%

PENALTIES SCORED
18

GOALS
94

KEY PASSES
289

CLEARANCES
2,804

TACKLES
1,373

MAJOR CLUB HONORS
⚽ Ligue 1: 2022, 2023 (all PSG) ⚽ La Liga: 2007-08, 2012, 2017, 2020 (all R. Mad.) ⚽ UEFA Champions League: 2014, 2016, 2017, 2018 (all R. Mad.) ⚽ UEFA Super Cup: 2014, 2016, 2017 (all R. Mad.) ⚽ FIFA Club World Cup: 2014, 2016-18 (all R. Mad.)

INTERNATIONAL HONORS
⚽ FIFA World Cup: 2010
⚽ UEFA European Championship: 2008, 2012
⚽ FIFA Confederations Cup: Third place 2009, runner-up 2013

ACTIVITY AREAS

ANDREW ROBERTSON

In a short space of time, Andrew Robertson has become one of the world's best left-side defenders. He is fast and an excellent tackler and reader of the game, plus his ability to quickly run down the flank, complete neat one-twos, and whip over dangerous crosses makes him an asset in attack.

NATIONALITY
Scottish

CURRENT CLUB
Liverpool

26

DATE OF BIRTH	03/11/1994
POSITION	LEFT BACK
HEIGHT	5 FT. 10 IN.
WEIGHT	141 LB.
PREFERRED FOOT	LEFT

APPEARANCES
303

BLOCKS
58

INTERCEPTIONS
290

AERIAL DUELS WON
52%

PENALTIES SCORED
0

PASS COMPLETION
83%

GOALS
9

KEY PASSES
413

CLEARANCES
526

TACKLES
462

MAJOR CLUB HONORS
⚽ Premier League: 2020 ⚽ UEFA Champions League: 2019
⚽ FIFA World Club Cup: 2019 ⚽ UEFA Super Cup: 2019
⚽ FA Cup: 2022

INTERNATIONAL HONORS
⚽ None to date

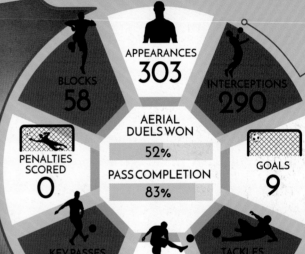

ACTIVITY AREAS

22

NATIONALITY
German

CURRENT CLUB
Real Madrid

ANTONIO RÜDIGER

Antonio Rüdiger has become a dominant defender all along the back line, winning tackles with his strength and dominating the penalty area with his heading ability. He is also an excellent passer, reads the game well, and leads by example.

DATE OF BIRTH	03/03/1993
POSITION	CENTER
HEIGHT	6 FT. 3¾ IN.
WEIGHT	187 LB.
PREFERRED FOOT	RIGHT

APPEARANCES
345

BLOCKS
126

INTERCEPTIONS
363

AERIAL DUELS WON
59%

PASS COMPLETION
87%

PENALTIES SCORED
0

GOALS
16

KEY PASSES
81

CLEARANCES
1,161

TACKLES
470

MAJOR CLUB HONORS
⚽ UEFA Champions League: 2021 (Chelsea) ⚽ FIFA World Club Cup: 2021 (Chelsea), 2022 ⚽ UEFA Europa League 2019 (Chelsea) ⚽ UEFA Super Cup: 2021 (Chelsea), 2022 ⚽ FA Cup: 2018 ⚽ Copa del Rey: 2023

INTERNATIONAL HONORS
⚽ FIFA Confederations Cup: 2017

ACTIVITY AREAS

STEFAN SAVIĆ

Stefan Savić reads the game well but his biggest strength is his ability in the air. He is comfortable on the ball and neat with his short passing, relying on brains instead of brawn to operate effectively at the back.

DATE OF BIRTH	01/08/1991
POSITION	CENTER
HEIGHT	6 FT. 1½ IN.
WEIGHT	179 LB.
PREFERRED FOOT	RIGHT

APPEARANCES
356

BLOCKS
205

INTERCEPTIONS
628

AERIAL DUELS WON
64%

PASS COMPLETION
85%

PENALTIES SCORED
0

GOALS
8

KEY PASSES
45

CLEARANCES
1,716

TACKLES
472

MAJOR CLUB HONORS
- La Liga: 2021
- UEFA Europa League: 2018
- UEFA Super Cup: 2018
- Premier League: 2012 (Man City)

INTERNATIONAL HONORS
- None to date

ACTIVITY AREAS

6

NATIONALITY
Brazilian

CURRENT CLUB
Chelsea

THIAGO SILVA

Players past and present rate Thiago Silva as one of the best center defenders to have played the game. In addition to his technical strengths, he is a natural leader who is able to inspire teammates to raise their game in the heat of battle.

DATE OF BIRTH	09/22/1984
POSITION	CENTER
HEIGHT	6 FT.
WEIGHT	174 LB.
PREFERRED FOOT	RIGHT

BLOCKS
334

APPEARANCES
484

INTERCEPTIONS
1,018

AERIAL DUELS WON
72%

PASS COMPLETION
93%

PENALTIES SCORED
0

GOALS
23

KEY PASSES
107

CLEARANCES
2,440

TACKLES
714

MAJOR CLUB HONORS
⚽ UEFA Champions League: 2021, runner-up 2020 (PSG) ⚽
UEFA Super Cup: 2021 ⚽ FIFA Club World Cup: 2021 ⚽
Serie A: 2011 (AC Milan) ⚽ Ligue 1: 2013-2020 (PSG) ⚽
Coupe de France: 2015-18, 2020 (all PSG) ⚽ FA Cup: 2022

INTERNATIONAL HONORS
⚽ FIFA Confederations Cup; 2013
⚽ Copa América: 2019, runner-up 2021

ACTIVITY AREAS

MILAN ŠKRINIAR

Centerback Milan Škriniar is a forceful tackler, strong in the air and combative on the ground. But what sets Škriniar apart are his ball-playing skills and his ability to stay calm under pressure and pick out intelligent passes.

NATIONALITY
Slovakian

CURRENT CLUB
Inter Milan

DATE OF BIRTH	02/11//1995
POSITION	CENTER
HEIGHT	6 FT. 1½ FT.
WEIGHT	176 LB.
PREFERRED FOOT	RIGHT

APPEARANCES
266

BLOCKS
181

INTERCEPTIONS
246

AERIAL DUELS WON
52%

PENALTIES SCORED
0

PASS COMPLETION
92%

GOALS
11

KEY PASSES
62

CLEARANCES
885

TACKLES
430

MAJOR CLUB HONORS
⚽ Serie A: 2021 ⚽ UEFA Champions League: Runner-up 2023 ⚽ UEFA Europa League: Runner-up 2020 ⚽ Coppa Italia: 2022, 2023

INTERNATIONAL HONORS
⚽ King's Cup: 2018

ACTIVITY AREAS

2

NATIONALITY
French

CURRENT CLUB
Bayern Munich

DAYOT UPAMECANO

Dayot Upamecano has developed into an exceptional centerback with all the talents needed for the position. His standout talent is his ability with the ball at his feet—a quality that complements his passing accuracy.

DATE OF BIRTH	10/27/1998
POSITION	CENTER
HEIGHT	6 FT. 1½ IN.
WEIGHT	183 LB.
PREFERRED FOOT	RIGHT

APPEARANCES
221

BLOCKS
82

INTERCEPTIONS
341

AERIAL DUELS WON
61%

PASS COMPLETION
88%

PENALTIES SCORED
0

GOALS
5

KEY PASSES
58

CLEARANCES
677

TACKLES
449

MAJOR CLUB HONORS
⚽ Bundesliga: 2022, 2023
⚽ DFL Supercup: 2021

INTERNATIONAL HONORS
⚽ UEFA Nations League: 2021
⚽ FIFA World Cup: Runner-up 2022

ACTIVITY AREAS

RAPHAËL VARANE

While most defenders peak in their late 20s, Raphaël Varane was already a star in his teens. Accurate with both feet, an excellent tackler, and great in the air, Varane can also launch attacks with his sharp passing and even score goals.

NATIONALITY
French

CURRENT CLUB
Manchester United

19

DATE OF BIRTH	04/25/1993
POSITION	CENTER
HEIGHT	6 FT. 3 IN.
WEIGHT	179 LB.
PREFERRED FOOT	RIGHT

APPEARANCES
398

BLOCKS
201

INTERCEPTIONS
546

AERIAL DUELS WON
70%

PASS COMPLETION
88%

PENALTIES SCORED
0

GOALS
13

KEY PASSES
67

CLEARANCES
1,719

TACKLES
460

MAJOR CLUB HONORS
⚽ La Liga: 2012, 2017, 2020 (R. Madrid) ⚽ UEFA Champions League: 2014, 2016, 2017, 2018 (R. Madrid) ⚽ UEFA Super Cup: 2014, 2016, 2017 (R. Madrid) ⚽ FIFA Club World Cup: 2014, 2016, 2017, 2018 (R. Madrid) ⚽ FA Cup: Runner-up 2023

INTERNATIONAL HONORS
⚽ FIFA World Cup: 2018, runner-up 2022
⚽ UEFA Nations League: 2021

ACTIVITY AREAS

MIDFIELDERS

Midfielders are the heartbeat of a team. Not only do they play between the forwards and the defenders but they also help out their teammates at both ends. Midfielders fall into one of four main categories: 1) defensive midfielders, who sit in front of the back four and are great tacklers; 2) the attacking fullbacks operating on the wings, who whip crosses into the box; 3) the center midfielders, who are great at setting up and then joining attacks, as well as helping out in defense whenever needed; and 4) the playmakers—these are the stars who build the attack with their creative play.

WHAT DO THE STATS MEAN?

ASSISTS
A pass, cross, or header to a teammate who then scores counts as an assist. This stat also includes a deflected shot that is converted by a teammate.

SHOTS
Any deliberate strike on goal counts as a shot. The strike does not have to be on target or force a save from the keeper.

CHANCES CREATED
Any pass that results in a shot at goal (whether or not the goal is scored) is regarded as a chance created.

TACKLES
This is the number of times the player has challenged and dispossessed the opposition without committing a foul.

DRIBBLES
This is the number of times the player has gone past an opponent while running with the ball.

75%
SUCCESSFUL PASSES
This shows, as a percentage, how successful the midfielder is at finding teammates with passes, whether more than 5 or 60 yards.

Did you know?

In top-level soccer, midfielders tend to cover the most ground during the course of a game. A midfielder playing the full 90 minutes will usually run between 6 and 7½ miles.

5

NATIONALITY
English

CURRENT CLUB
Real Madrid

JUDE BELLINGHAM

Jude Bellingham's talent was evident in 2019, when he was just 16 years old! Now he has fulfilled that promise and become one of the world's best midfielders. He is a good tackler, exceptionally quick, positionally aware, and his vision allows him to create and score goals.

DATE OF BIRTH	06/29/2003
POSITION	CENTER
HEIGHT	6 FT. 1½ IN.
WEIGHT	165 LB.
PREFERRED FOOT	RIGHT

APPEARANCES
117

ASSISTS
21

DRIBBLES
367

PASSES
5,179

SUCCESSFUL PASSES
84%

PENALTIES SCORED
1

GOALS
20

SHOTS
185

CHANCES CREATED
112

TACKLES
234

MAJOR CLUB HONORS
⚽ Bundesliga: Runner-up 2023 (Borussia Dortmund)
⚽ DFB-Pukal: 2021 (Borussia Dortmund)

INTERNATIONAL HONORS
⚽ UEFA European Championship: Runner-up 2021

ACTIVITY AREAS

KEVIN DE BRUYNE

Kevin De Bruyne ranks as one of the finest attacking midfielders in the game today. Strong and technically brilliant, he can break up play at one end and almost immediately blast a 25-yard shot into the opposite goal.

NATIONALITY
Belgian

CURRENT CLUB
Manchester City

DATE OF BIRTH	06/28/1991
POSITION	ATTACKING
HEIGHT	5 FT. 11¼ IN.
WEIGHT	150 LB.
PREFERRED FOOT	RIGHT

APPEARANCES
408

ASSISTS
166

DRIBBLES
1,209

PASSES
19,677

SUCCESSFUL PASSES
80%

PENALTIES SCORED
5

GOALS
106

SHOTS
978

CHANCES CREATED
1,183

TACKLES
490

MAJOR CLUB HONORS
- Premier League: 2018, 2019, 2021, 2022, 2023
- UEFA Champions League: Runner-up 2021, 2023
- FA Cup: 2019, 2023

INTERNATIONAL HONORS
- FIFA World Cup: Third place 2018

ACTIVITY AREAS

*At Barcelona

NATIONALITY
Spanish

CURRENT CLUB
TBC

SERGIO BUSQUETS

Sergio Busquets plays as a deep midfielder who dictates the team's build-up play with clever, short and long passes. He is great at stopping attacks before they become dangerous and then making passes to launch his team's raids.

DATE OF BIRTH	07/16/1988
POSITION	DEFENSIVE
HEIGHT	6 FT. 2¼ IN.
WEIGHT	168 LB.
PREFERRED FOOT	RIGHT

ASSISTS
40

APPEARANCES
617

DRIBBLES
426

PASSES
44100
SUCCESSFUL PASSES
91%

PENALTIES SCORED
0

GOALS
16

SHOTS
152

CHANCES CREATED
389

TACKLES
1,576

MAJOR CLUB HONORS
⚽ La Liga: 2009-11, 2013, 2015 2016, 2018, 2019, 2023 (All Barca) ⚽ UEFA Champions League: 2009, 2011, 2015 (all Barca) ⚽ UEFA Super Cup: 2009, 2011, 2015 (all Barca) ⚽ FIFA Club World Cup: 2009, 2011, 2015 (all barca)

INTERNATIONAL HONORS
⚽ FIFA World Cup: 2010 ⚽ UEFA European Championship: 2012 ⚽ FIFA Confederations Cup: Runner-up 2013 ⚽ UEFA Nations League: Runner-up 2021

ACTIVITY AREAS

EMRE CAN

Having been a defender earlier in his career, Emre Can has grown into a classy center midfielder. He combines his excellent tackling strength with his midfielder's instincts to thread passes to teammates in attacking positions.

NATIONALITY
German

CURRENT CLUB
Borussia Dortmund

23

DATE OF BIRTH	01/12/1994
POSITION	CENTER
HEIGHT	6 FT. 1¼ IN.
WEIGHT	189 LB.
PREFERRED FOOT	RIGHT

APPEARANCES
333

ASSISTS
18

DRIBBLES
584

PASSES
16,389

PENALTIES
SCORED
6

SUCCESSFUL
PASSES
85%

GOALS
30

SHOTS
305

CHANCES
CREATED
211

TACKLES
720

MAJOR CLUB HONORS

⚽ Bundesliga: 2013 (B. Mun.), runner-up 2023 ⚽ UEFA Champions League: 2013 (B. Mun.), runner-up 2018 (Liverpool) ⚽ UEFA Europa League: Runner-up 2016 (Liverpool) ⚽ Serie A: 2019, 2020 (Juventus) ⚽ DFB-Pokal: 2013 (B. Mun), 2021

INTERNATIONAL HONORS

⚽ FIFA Confederations Cup: 2017

ACTIVITY AREAS

18

NATIONALITY
Brazilian

CURRENT CLUB
Manchester United

CASEMIRO

Casemiro's strengths are great energy, a high work rate, and good support play. Strong, mobile, and hard-tackling, his best position is as a defensive midfielder, although his mobility helps him get from box to box and he can also play at centerback.

DATE OF BIRTH	02/23/1992
POSITION	CENTER
HEIGHT	6 FT. ¾ IN.
WEIGHT	185 LB.
PREFERRED FOOT	RIGHT

ASSISTS
26

APPEARANCES
343

DRIBBLES
253

PASSES
18,255
SUCCESSFUL PASSES
85%

PENALTIES SCORED
0

GOALS
35

SHOTS
385

CHANCES CREATED
219

TACKLES
1,038

MAJOR CLUB HONORS
⚽ La Liga: 2017, 2020, 2022 (all R. Mad) ⚽ UEFA Champs League: 2014, 2016, 2017, 2018, 2022 (all R. Mad) ⚽ UEFA Super Cup: 2016, 2017, 2022 (all R. Mad) ⚽ FIFA Club World Cup: 2016, 2017, 2018 (all R. Mad) ⚽ FA Cup: Runner-up 2023

INTERNATIONAL HONORS
⚽ FIFA U-20 World Cup: 2011
⚽ Copa América: 2019, runner-up 2021

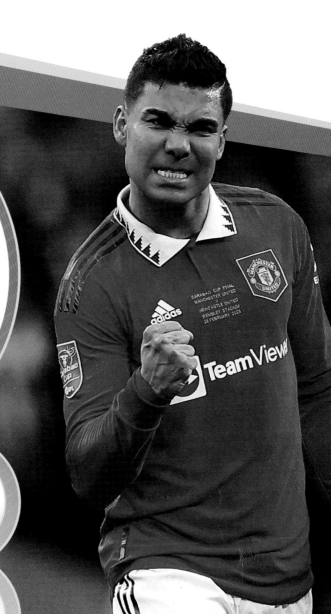

ACTIVITY AREAS

PHILIPPE COUTINHO

Philippe Coutinho brings Brazilian flair to the proceedings whenever he steps onto the field. Highly skilled with both feet, he is the type of attacking midfielder opposition defenders hate to face in one-to-one situations.

NATIONALITY
Brazilian

CURRENT CLUB
Aston Villa

DATE OF BIRTH	06/12/1992
POSITION	ATTACKING
HEIGHT	5 FT. 7¾ IN.
WEIGHT	150 LB.
PREFERRED FOOT	RIGHT

ASSISTS
67

APPEARANCES
401

DRIBBLES
1,399

PASSES
14,812

SUCCESSFUL PASSES
82%

PENALTIES SCORED
3

GOALS
95

SHOTS
1,038

CHANCES CREATED
578

TACKLES
453

MAJOR CLUB HONORS

⚽ Bundesliga: 2020 (Bayern Munich) ⚽ La Liga: 2018, 2019 (Barcelona) ⚽ UEFA Champions League: 2020 (B. Munich) ⚽ DFB-Pokal: 2020 (Bayern Munich) ⚽ Copa del Rey: 2018, 2021 (Barcelona) ⚽ Copa Italia: 2011 (Inter Milan)

INTERNATIONAL HONORS

⚽ Copa América: 2019
⚽ FIFA U-20 World Cup: 2011

ACTIVITY AREAS

3

NATIONALITY
Brazilian

CURRENT CLUB
Liverpool

FABINHO

A hard worker in front of defense, Fabinho is a fan favorite at Liverpool in England. Tall and strong, he is a master at keeping possession for his team and starting the attack from deep. His heat map shows how dominant he is in midfield.

DATE OF BIRTH	10/23/1993
POSITION	DEFENSIVE
HEIGHT	6 FT. 2 IN.
WEIGHT	172 LB.
PREFERRED FOOT	RIGHT

APPEARANCES
396

ASSISTS
21

DRIBBLES
426

PASSES
20,282

SUCCESSFUL PASSES
86%

PENALTIES SCORED
19

GOALS
34

SHOTS
221

CHANCES CREATED
240

TACKLES
992

MAJOR CLUB HONORS
⚽ Premier League: 2020 ⚽ UEFA Champions League: 2019
⚽ UEFA Super Cup: 2019 ⚽ FIFA Club World Cup: 2019
⚽ Ligue 1: 2017 (Monaco) ⚽ FA Cup: 2022

INTERNATIONAL HONORS
⚽ Copa América: 2019, runner-up 2021

ACTIVITY AREAS

BRUNO FERNANDES

Bruno Fernandes shines as a center or attacking midfielder. A sound defensive player, he has a fantastic eye for creating chances with through balls, driving powerful shots from long range, and is superb with penalties and free kicks.

NATIONALITY
Portuguese

CURRENT CLUB
Manchester United

8

DATE OF BIRTH	09/08/1994
POSITION	ATTACKING
HEIGHT	5 FT. 10½ IN.
WEIGHT	152 LB.
PREFERRED FOOT	RIGHT

ASSISTS
69

APPEARANCES
306

DRIBBLES
540

PENALTIES SCORED
26

PASSES
12,974

SUCCESSFUL PASSES
77%

GOALS
84

SHOTS
742

CHANCES CREATED
647

TACKLES
453

MAJOR CLUB HONORS
⚽ UEFA Europa League: Runner-up 2021 ⚽ Taça de Portugal: 2019 (Sporting CP) ⚽ Taça de Liga: 2018, 2019 (Sporting CP) ⚽ FA Cup: Runner-up 2023

INTERNATIONAL HONORS
⚽ UEFA Nations League: 2019

ACTIVITY AREAS

5

NATIONALITY
Argentinian

CURRENT CLUB
Chelsea

ENZO FERNÁNDEZ

Enzo Fernandez has enjoyed a meteoric rise, highlighted by his award as FIFA Best Young Player at the 2022 World Cup. Playing in center midfield, he is happy to help his defenders, while his exceptionally accurate long-range passing often launches dangerous attacks.

DATE OF BIRTH	01/17/2001
POSITION	CENTER
HEIGHT	5 FT. 10 IN.
WEIGHT	168 LB.
PREFERRED FOOT	RIGHT

ASSISTS
3

APPEARANCES
27

DRIBBLES
41

PENALTIES SCORED
0

PASSES
2,009
SUCCESSFUL PASSES
89%

GOALS
0

SHOTS
39

CHANCES CREATED
26

TACKLES
72

MAJOR CLUB HONORS
⚽ Argentina Primera División: 2021 (River Plate)

INTERNATIONAL HONORS
⚽ FIFA World Cup: 2022

ACTIVITY AREAS

42

ROBERTO FIRMINO

Roberto Firmino is a box-to-box midfielder with great energy and a perfect passing technique over both long and short distances. He usually plays as a second attacker with a superb left foot, but also surprises defenders with his heading ability.

NATIONALITY
Brazilian

CURRENT CLUB
TBC

9*

*At Liverpool

DATE OF BIRTH	10/02/1991
POSITION	ATT/STRIKER
HEIGHT	5 FT. 11¼ IN.
WEIGHT	168 LB.
PREFERRED FOOT	RIGHT

APPEARANCES
466

ASSISTS
88

DRIBBLES
1,661

PASSES
15,496

SUCCESSFUL PASSES
77%

PENALTIES SCORED
5

GOALS
143

SHOTS
1,033

CHANCES CREATED
688

TACKLES
805

MAJOR CLUB HONORS
⚽ Premier League: 2020 (Liv'pool) ⚽ UEFA Champ. League: 2019, runner-up 2022 (all Liv'pool) ⚽ UEFA Europa League: Runner-up 2016 (Liv'pool) ⚽ UEFA Super Cup: 2019 (Liv'pool) ⚽ FIFA Club World Cup: 2019 (Liv'pool) ⚽ FA Cup: 2022 (Liv'pool)

INTERNATIONAL HONORS
⚽ Copa América: 2019, runner-up 2021

ACTIVITY AREAS

10

NATIONALITY
English

CURRENT CLUB
Manchester City

JACK GREALISH

Jack Grealish is among the finest attacking midfielders in Europe. He displays tight ball control, dribbling ability, change of speed, and can shoot or deliver dangerous balls into the penalty area from the right or center positions.

DATE OF BIRTH	05/10/1995
POSITION	ATTACKING
HEIGHT	5 FT. 9 IN.
WEIGHT	168 LB.
PREFERRED FOOT	RIGHT

ASSISTS
29

APPEARANCES
170

DRIBBLES
538

PASSES
5,676

SUCCESSFUL PASSES
86%

PENALTIES SCORED
0

GOALS
24

SHOTS
264

CHANCES CREATED
353

TACKLES
136

MAJOR CLUB HONORS
⚽ Premier League: 2022, 2023 ⚽ UEFA Champions League: 2023 ⚽ FA Cup: Runner-up 2015 (Aston Villa), 2023

INTERNATIONAL HONORS
⚽ UEFA European Championship: Runner-up 2020

ACTIVITY AREAS

FRENKIE DE JONG

Frenkie de Jong has been an outstanding talent ever since he burst onto the scene as a teenager. His close control, accuracy, work rate, passing accuracy, and movement have seen him being compared to the great Johan Cruyff.

DATE OF BIRTH	05/12/1997
POSITION	CENTER
HEIGHT	5 FT. 10¾ IN.
WEIGHT	163 LB.
PREFERRED FOOT	RIGHT

APPEARANCES
180

ASSISTS
16

DRIBBLES
332

PASSES
11,115

PENALTIES SCORED
0

SUCCESSFUL PASSES
91%

GOALS
11

SHOTS
73

CHANCES CREATED
197

TACKLES
229

MAJOR CLUB HONORS
⚽ La Liga: 2023 ⚽ UEFA Europa League: Runner-up 2017 (Ajax) ⚽ Copa del Rey: 2021 ⚽ Eredivisie: 2019 (Ajax) ⚽ KNVB Cup: 2019 (Ajax)

INTERNATIONAL HONORS
⚽ UEFA Nations League: Runner-up: 2019

ACTIVITY AREAS

20

NATIONALITY
Italian

CURRENT CLUB
Arsenal

JORGINHO

The talented Jorginho can control the tempo of play from deep, link defense with midfield, and midfield with attack with his accurate passing. He has the awareness, vision, and passing ability to break lines, and he can deliver lofted balls to attacking teammates.

DATE OF BIRTH	12/20/1991
POSITION	DEFENSIVE
HEIGHT	5 FT. 10¾ IN.
WEIGHT	143 LB.
PREFERRED FOOT	BOTH

ASSISTS
26

APPEARANCES
369

DRIBBLES
286

PASSES
27,193

SUCCESSFUL
PASSES
89%

PENALTIES
SCORED
32

GOALS
37

SHOTS
167

CHANCES
CREATED
379

TACKLES
759

MAJOR CLUB HONORS
⚽ Prem. League: Runner-up 2023 ⚽ UEFA Champs League: 2021 (Chelsea) ⚽ UEFA Europa League: 2019 (Chelsea) ⚽ FIFA World Club Cup: 2021 (Chelsea) ⚽ UEFA Super Cup: 2021 (Chelsea) ⚽ FA Cup: Runner-up 2020-22 (Chelsea) ⚽ Coppa Italia: 2014 (Napoli)

INTERNATIONAL HONORS
⚽ UEFA European Championship: 2020
⚽ UEFA Nations League: Third place 2021, third place 2023

ACTIVITY AREAS

N'GOLO KANTÉ

Defensive midfielder N'Golo Kanté has pace to burn, boundless energy, and great positional awareness. He frequently breaks up attacks with timely tackles, blocks, and interceptions, then makes accurate passes. He has a decent eye for goal, too.

NATIONALITY
French

CURRENT CLUB
Chelsea

DATE OF BIRTH	03/29/1991
POSITION	CENTER
HEIGHT	5 FT. 6 IN.
WEIGHT	150 LB.
PREFERRED FOOT	RIGHT

APPEARANCES
305

ASSISTS
24

DRIBBLES
608

PENALTIES SCORED
0

PASSES
15,191

SUCCESSFUL PASSES
86%

GOALS
14

SHOTS
207

CHANCES CREATED
303

TACKLES
934

MAJOR CLUB HONORS
⚽ Premier League: 2016 (Leicester City), 2017 ⚽ UEFA Champions League: 2021 ⚽ UEFA Europa League: 2019 ⚽ FIFA Club World Cup: 2021 ⚽ UEFA Super Cup: 2021 ⚽ FA Cup: 2018, runner-up 2020-22

INTERNATIONAL HONORS
⚽ FIFA World Cup: 2018
⚽ UEFA European Championship: Runner-up 2016

ACTIVITY AREAS

47

8

CURRENT CLUB
Real Madrid

TONI KROOS

A set piece specialist who wins challenges in both boxes and dictates the game, Toni Kroos is an athletic box-to-box midfielder who can can pass long and short with either foot. He possesses great vision, creativity, and energy.

DATE OF BIRTH	01/04/1990
POSITION	CENTER
HEIGHT	6 FT.
WEIGHT	168 LB.
PREFERRED FOOT	RIGHT

APPEARANCES
591

ASSISTS
119

DRIBBLES
639

PENALTIES SCORED
0

PASSES
37,649
SUCCESSFUL PASSES
92%

GOALS
56

SHOTS
849

CHANCES CREATED
1,195

TACKLES
1,086

MAJOR CLUB HONORS
⚽ La Liga: 2017, 2020, 2022 ⚽ Bund'liga: 2008, 2013-14 (all B. Mun.) ⚽ UEFA Champs L.: 2013 (B. Mun.), 2016-18, 2022 ⚽ FIFA Club WC: 2013 (B. Mun.), 2014, 2016-18, 2022 ⚽ UEFA Sup. Cup: 2013 (B. Mun), 2014, 2017, 2022 ⚽ Copa del Rey: 2023

INTERNATIONAL HONORS
⚽ FIFA World Cup: 2014

ACTIVITY AREAS

48

SERGEJ MILINKOVIĆ-SAVIĆ

Effective in and around both penalty areas, Sergej Milinković-Savić is a top-class midfielder. He is blessed with great energy and sound technique, and he's also good at stopping opposition attacks and launching his own team's raids.

NATIONALITY
Serbian

CURRENT CLUB
Lazio

21

DATE OF BIRTH	02/27/1995
POSITION	CENTER
HEIGHT	6 FT. 3 IN.
WEIGHT	181 LB.
PREFERRED FOOT	RIGHT

APPEARANCES
312

ASSISTS
50

DRIBBLES
663

PENALTIES SCORED
0

PASSES
14,806
SUCCESSFUL PASSES
77%

GOALS
64

SHOTS
631

CHANCES CREATED
396

TACKLES
502

MAJOR CLUB HONORS
⚽ Serie A: Runner-up 2023   ⚽ Coppa Italia: 2019

INTERNATIONAL HONORS
⚽ UEFA European U-19 Championship: 2013
⚽ FIFA U-20 World Cup: 2015

ACTIVITY AREAS

10

NATIONALITY
Croatian

CURRENT CLUB
Real Madrid

LUKA MODRIĆ

Playmaker Luka Modrić is often at the heart of his team's best attacking moves. He has a great brain for soccer, can deliver long and short passes with both feet, and can strike powerful long-range shots, especially free kicks.

DATE OF BIRTH	09/09/1985
POSITION	ATTACKING
HEIGHT	5 FT. 7³/₄ IN.
WEIGHT	146 LB.
PREFERRED FOOT	RIGHT

ASSISTS
84

APPEARANCES
585

DRIBBLES
1,419

PENALTIES SCORED
6

PASSES
32,544
SUCCESSFUL PASSES
89%

GOALS
51

SHOTS
705

CHANCES CREATED
896

TACKLES
767

MAJOR CLUB HONORS

⚽ La Liga: 2017, 2020, 2022, runner-up 2023 ⚽ UEFA Champions League: 2014, 2016, 2017, 2018, 2022 ⚽ UEFA Super Cup: 2014, 2016, 2017, 2022 ⚽ FIFA Club World Cup: 2014, 2016, 2017, 2018, 2022 ⚽ Copa del Rey: 2023

INTERNATIONAL HONORS

⚽ FIFA World Cup: Runner-up 2018, third place 2022
⚽ UEFA Nations League: Runner-up

ACTIVITY AREAS

THOMAS MÜLLER

Thomas Müller is a dangerous attacking midfielder who scores countless goals playing just behind a lone striker. The German powerhouse is mentally strong, tactically clever, and great at finding holes in the opposition's defense.

NATIONALITY
German

CURRENT CLUB
Bayern Munich

25

DATE OF BIRTH	09/13/1989
POSITION	SECOND STRIKER
HEIGHT	6 FT. ¾ IN.
WEIGHT	168 LB.
PREFERRED FOOT	RIGHT

ASSISTS
183

APPEARANCES
584

DRIBBLES
1,022

PENALTIES SCORED
22

PASSES
19,122

SUCCESSFUL PASSES
77%

GOALS
197

SHOTS
1,153

CHANCES CREATED
1,103

TACKLES
614

MAJOR CLUB HONORS
⚽ Bundesliga: (12 times) 2010–2023
⚽ UEFA Champions League: 2013, 2020
⚽ UEFA Super Cup: 2013, 2020
⚽ FIFA Club World Cup: 2013, 2020

INTERNATIONAL HONORS
⚽ FIFA World Cup: 2014, third place 2010

ACTIVITY AREAS

10

NATIONALITY
American

CURRENT CLUB
Chelsea

CHRISTIAN PULISIC

Although capable of playing in any attacking position, Christian Pulisic's pace, agility, and technical ability have made him most effective on the left wing. He also likes to have the ball at his feet, dribbling past opponents to create shooting opportunities for himself.

DATE OF BIRTH	09/18/1998
POSITION	RIGHT
HEIGHT	5 FT. 10½ IN.
WEIGHT	152 LB.
PREFERRED FOOT	RIGHT

ASSISTS
32

APPEARANCES
242

DRIBBLES
998

PENALTIES SCORED
0

PASSES
5,161

SUCCESSFUL PASSES
80%

GOALS
40

SHOTS
324

CHANCES CREATED
219

TACKLES
206

MAJOR CLUB HONORS
⚽ UEFA Champions League: 2021 ⚽ UEFA Super Cup: 2021
⚽ FIFA Club World Cup: 2021 ⚽ FA Cup: 2020, 2021, 2022
(all runner-up) ⚽ DFB-Pokal: 2017 (Borussia Dortmund)

INTERNATIONAL HONORS
⚽ CONCACAF Nations League: 2020
⚽ ONCACAF Gold Cup: 2019: Runner-up

ACTIVITY AREAS

BUKAYO SAKA

A rising star in world soccer, Buyako Saka's versatility is just one of his talents. Equally good on both sides at fullback or winger, his creativity, positional sense, tackling, shooting, and passing talents are displayed best as a right midfielder.

NATIONALITY
English

CURRENT CLUB
Arsenal

DATE OF BIRTH	09/05/2001
POSITION	WINGER
HEIGHT	5 FT. 10 IN.
WEIGHT	159 LB.
PREFERRED FOOT	LEFT

APPEARANCES 160

ASSISTS 34

DRIBBLES 496

PENALTIES SCORED 4

PASSES 4,595
SUCCESSFUL PASSES 81%

GOALS 36

SHOTS 298

CHANCES CREATED 237

TACKLES 186

MAJOR CLUB HONORS
⚽ Premier League: Runner-up 2023 ⚽ FA Cup: 2020
⚽ UEFA Europa League: Runner-up 2019

INTERNATIONAL HONORS
⚽ UEFA European Championship: Runner-up 2020 (2021)

ACTIVITY AREAS

18

NATIONALITY
Portuguese

CURRENT CLUB
Paris Saint-Germain

RENATO SANCHES

Renato Sanches can play in almost every midfield position: defensive, wide, center, or as a creative playmaker. Calm in possession, he is a fine passer and strong tackler, and he is not afraid of shooting from distance.

DATE OF BIRTH	08/18/1997
POSITION	CENTER
HEIGHT	5 FT. 9¼ IN.
WEIGHT	154 LB.
PREFERRED FOOT	RIGHT

ASSISTS 10

APPEARANCES 172

DRIBBLES 442

PENALTIES SCORED 0

PASSES 5,930
SUCCESSFUL PASSES 86%

GOALS 10

SHOTS 152

CHANCES CREATED 133

TACKLES 125

MAJOR CLUB HONORS
- Ligue 1: 2021 (Lille), 2023
- Bundesliga: 2017, 2019 (Bayern Munich)
- DFB-Pokal: 2019 (Bayern Munich)
- Premeira Liga: 2016 (Benfica)

INTERNATIONAL HONORS
- UEFA European Championship: 2016

ACTIVITY AREAS

MARCO VERRATTI

Marco Verratti is an awesome ball-playing midfielder. He is able to dribble past defenders at speed to set up chances for the players ahead of him. He can pass or shoot accurately and powerfully with both feet.

NATIONALITY
Italian

CURRENT CLUB
Paris Saint-Germain

DATE OF BIRTH	11/05/1992
POSITION	CENTER
HEIGHT	5 FT. 5 IN.
WEIGHT	132 LB.
PREFERRED FOOT	RIGHT

ASSISTS
47

APPEARANCES
355

DRIBBLES
694

PENALTIES SCORED
0

PASSES
29,334

SUCCESSFUL PASSES
91%

GOALS
10

SHOTS
102

CHANCES CREATED
399

TACKLES
981

MAJOR CLUB HONORS
- Ligue 1: 2013, 2014-16, 2018-20, 2022, 2023
- UEFA Champions League: Runner-up 2020
- Coupe de France: 2015, 2016, 2017, 2018, 2020, 2021

INTERNATIONAL HONORS
- UEFA European Championship: 2020 ⚽ UEFA Nations League: Third place 2021, third place 2023

ACTIVITY AREAS

18

NATIONALITY
Dutch

CURRENT CLUB
Roma

GEORGINIO WIJNALDUM

Georginio Wijnaldum can play anywhere in the middle of the field as an attacking playmaker or a defensive shield for the back line. Good with both feet and a strong tackler, he goes box to box and scores crucial goals, especially with headers.

DATE OF BIRTH	11/11/1990
POSITION	CENTER
HEIGHT	56 FT. 9 IN.
WEIGHT	152 LB.
PREFERRED FOOT	RIGHT

ASSISTS
21

APPEARANCES
344

DRIBBLES
596

PENALTIES SCORED
2

PASSES
12,836
SUCCESSFUL PASSES
89%

GOALS
44

SHOTS
378

CHANCES CREATED
249

TACKLES
309

MAJOR CLUB HONORS
⚽ Ligue 1: 2022 (PSG) ⚽ Premier League: 2020 (Liv'pool)
⚽ UEFA Champions League: 2019 (Liv'pool), runner-up 2018 (Liv'pool) ⚽ Europa League: Runner-up 2023 ⚽ UEFA Super Cup: 2019 (Liv'pool) ⚽ FIFA Club World Cup: 2019 (Liv'pool)

INTERNATIONAL HONORS
⚽ UEFA Nations League: Runner-up: 2019
⚽ FIFA World Cup: Third place 2014

ACTIVITY AREAS

AXEL WITSEL

Originally a pacy right winger, Axel Witsel has developed into a strong center midfielder. He frequently drives his team forward with both his play and leadership skills. He is especially good at delivering dangerous passes with either foot.

NATIONALITY
Belgian

CURRENT CLUB
Atlético Madrid

20

DATE OF BIRTH	01/12/1989
POSITION	CENTER
HEIGHT	6 FT. 1¼ IN.
WEIGHT	179 LB.
PREFERRED FOOT	RIGHT

APPEARANCES
244

ASSISTS
11

DRIBBLES
215

PENALTIES SCORED
1

PASSES
13,015

SUCCESSFUL PASSES
92%

GOALS
20

SHOTS
200

CHANCES CREATED
111

TACKLES
384

MAJOR CLUB HONORS
⚽ DFL-Pokal: 2021 (Borussia Dortmund)
⚽ DFL-Supercup: 2019 (Borussia Dortmund)

INTERNATIONAL HONORS
⚽ FIFA World Cup: Third place 2018

ACTIVITY AREAS

FORWARDS

The forwards, or strikers, are a team's frontline attackers and the chief goal scorers. They are also the team's most celebrated players. Whether it is the smaller, quicker player, such as Neymar Jr. and Mohamed Salah, or the bigger, more physical attacker, such as Erling Haaland and Romelu Lukaku, strikers have perfected the art of finding the back of the net on a regular basis. Aside from scoring a lot of goals, the world's best strikers are also effective at creating chances for their teammates.

WHAT DO THE STATS MEAN?

GOALS
This is the total number of goals a striker has scored. The figure spans across all the top clubs the player has represented so far in their career.

CONVERSION RATE
The percentage shows how good the player is at taking their chance in front of goal. If a player scores two goals from four shots, their conversion rate is 50 percent.

75%

ASSISTS
A pass, cross, or header to a teammate who then scores counts as an assist. This stat also includes a deflected shot that is immediately converted by a teammate.

MINUTES PER GOAL
This is the average length of time it takes for the player to score. It is calculated across all the minutes the player has played in their career at top level.

128

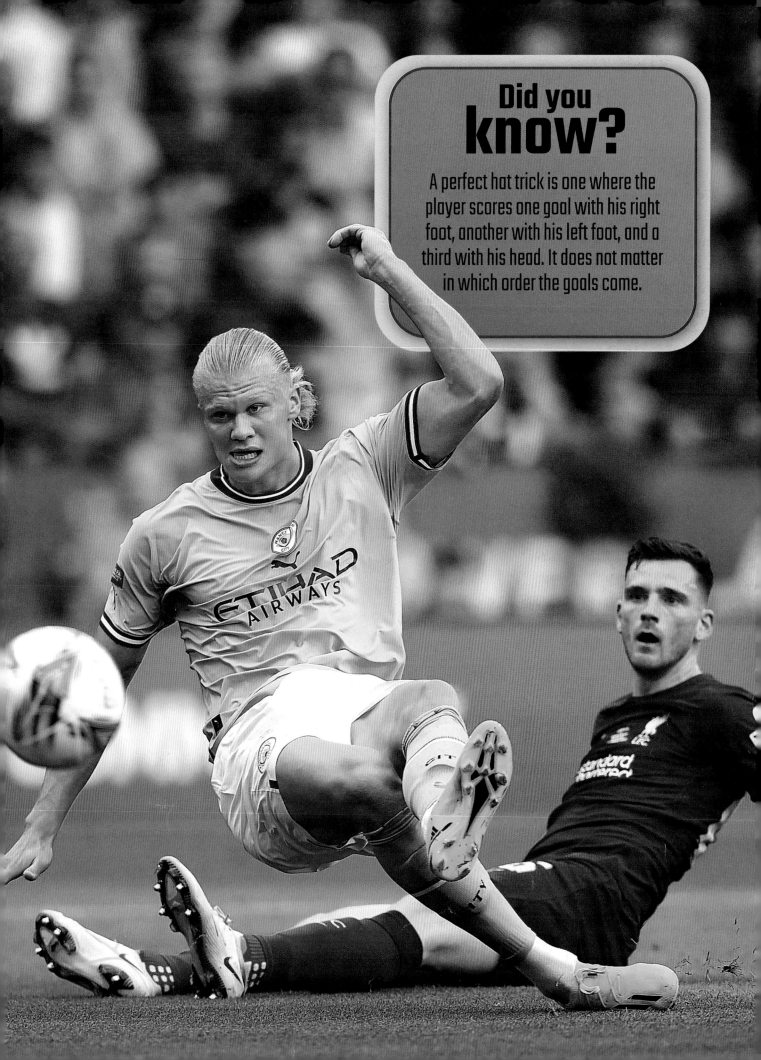

Did you know?

A perfect hat trick is one where the player scores one goal with his right foot, another with his left foot, and a third with his head. It does not matter in which order the goals come.

9*

*At Real Madrid

NATIONALITY
French

CURRENT CLUB
TBC

KARIM BENZEMA

Karim Benzema is both a creator and scorer of goals. Intelligent with a great work rate, he can play out wide, down the middle, or behind the front man. Although right-footed, he scores many goals with his left and his head.

DATE OF BIRTH	12/19/1987
POSITION	STRIKER
HEIGHT	6 FT. ¾ IN.
WEIGHT	179 LB.
PREFERRED FOOT	BOTH

GOALS
371

PENALTIES SCORED
31

APPEARANCES
703

ASSISTS
143

CONVERSION RATE
18.3%

MINUTES PER GOAL
136

GOALS LEFT
70

GOALS RIGHT
238

HAT TRICKS
10

HEADED GOALS
58

SHOTS
2,026

MAJOR CLUB HONORS
⚽ La Liga: 2012, '17, '20, '22 (R. Mad.) ⚽ UEFA C. League: 2014, 2016-18, '22 (R. Mad) ⚽ FIFA Club WC: 2014, 2016-18, '22 (R. Mad.) ⚽ UEFA S. Cup: 2014, 2016-17, '22 (R. Mad.) ⚽ Ligue 1: 2005-08 (Lyon) ⚽ Copa del Rey: 2023 (R. Mad.)

INTERNATIONAL HONORS
⚽ UEFA Nations League: 2021
⚽ FIFA World Cup: Runner-up 2022

ACTIVITY AREAS

EDINSON CAVANI

Edinson Cavani is a fine dribbler who is great at running into space and scoring spectacular goals, especially with overhead kicks. He has an impressive work rate, too, always hassling the opposition's defense to win the ball.

NATIONALITY
Uruguayan

CURRENT CLUB
TBC

7*

*At Valencia

DATE OF BIRTH	02/14/1987
POSITION	STRIKER
HEIGHT	6 FT. ½ IN.
WEIGHT	157 LB.
PREFERRED FOOT	RIGHT

GOALS
320

PENALTIES SCORED
47

ASSISTS
58

APPEARANCES
571

CONVERSION RATE
19.7%

MINUTES PER GOAL
132

GOALS LEFT
50

GOALS RIGHT
211

HAT TRICKS
14

HEADED GOALS
56

SHOTS
1,625

MAJOR CLUB HONORS
- UEFA Champions League: Runner-up 2020 (PSG)
- UEFA Europa League: Runner-up 2021 (Man Utd)
- Ligue 1: 2014, 2015, 2016, 2018, 2019, 2020 (all PSG)
- Coupe de France: 2015, 2016, 2017, 2018, 2020 (all PSG)

INTERNATIONAL HONORS
- Copa América: 2011

ACTIVITY AREAS

NATIONALITY
Dutch

CURRENT CLUB
Atlético Madrid

MEMPHIS DEPAY

Memphis Depay has developed into a world-class striker, although he is still considered to be a left winger or left-side striker. He is a brave player and will challenge the biggest defenders in the middle of the danger area.

DATE OF BIRTH	02/13/1994
POSITION	WINGER
HEIGHT	5 FT. 10 IN.
WEIGHT	172 LB.
PREFERRED FOOT	RIGHT

GOALS 100
PENALTIES SCORED 19
APPEARANCES 273
ASSISTS 55
CONVERSION RATE 14%
MINUTES PER GOAL 184
GOALS LEFT 18
GOALS RIGHT 79
HAT TRICKS 3
HEADED GOALS 3
SHOTS 714

MAJOR CLUB HONORS
⚽ Eredivisie: 2015 (PSV Eindhoven) ⚽ KNVB Cup: 2012 (PSV Eindhoven) ⚽ FA Cup: 2016 (Manchester United)

INTERNATIONAL HONORS
⚽ FIFA World Cup: Third place 2014

ACTIVITY AREAS

JOÃO FÉLIX

The latest star striker to emerge out of Portugal, João Félix perfected his craft in *La Liga* before making a loan move to the Premier League in 2023. An eye for goal combined with versatility mean he can be deployed as a center striker, second forward, attacking midfielder, or winger.

NATIONALITY
Portuguese

CURRENT CLUB
TBC

11*

*At Chelsea

DATE OF BIRTH	11/10/1999
POSITION	FORWARD
HEIGHT	5 FT. 11¼ IN.
WEIGHT	154 LB.
PREFERRED FOOT	RIGHT

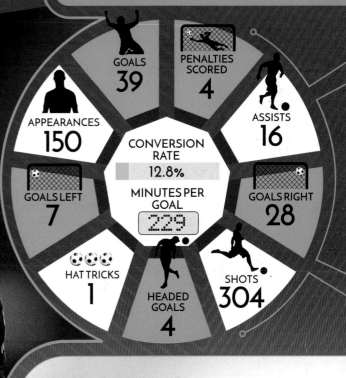

GOALS
39

PENALTIES SCORED
4

ASSISTS
16

APPEARANCES
150

CONVERSION RATE
12.8%

MINUTES PER GOAL
229

GOALS LEFT
7

GOALS RIGHT
28

HAT TRICKS
1

HEADED GOALS
4

SHOTS
304

MAJOR CLUB HONORS
- La Liga: 2021 (Atlético Madrid)
- Primeira Liga: 2019 (Benfica)

INTERNATIONAL HONORS
- UEFA Nations League: 2019

ACTIVITY AREAS

NATIONALITY
French

CURRENT CLUB
AC Milan

OLIVIER GIROUD

Olivier Giroud is much more than a target man, because his work rate and positional sense make him hard to defend against near the goal. He uses his physique to hold and shield the ball, and he is known for his accurate passing, shooting, and heading.

DATE OF BIRTH	09/30/1986
POSITION	STRIKER
HEIGHT	6 FT. 4 IN.
WEIGHT	200 LB.
PREFERRED FOOT	LEFT

GOALS
184

PENALTIES SCORED
19

ASSISTS
61

APPEARANCES
468

CONVERSION RATE
15.9%

MINUTES PER GOAL
162

GOALS LEFT
113

GOALS RIGHT
18

HAT TRICKS
7

HEADED GOALS
53

SHOTS
1,154

MAJOR CLUB HONORS

⚽ Serie A: 2022 ⚽ UEFA Champions League: 2021 (Chelsea) ⚽ UEFA Europa League: 2019 (Chelsea) ⚽ Ligue 1: 2012 (Montpellier) ⚽ FA Cup: 2014, 2015, 2017 (Arsenal), 2018 (Chelsea)

INTERNATIONAL HONORS

⚽ FIFA World Cup 2018, runner-up 2022
⚽ UEFA European Championship: Runner-up 2016

ACTIVITY AREAS

ANTOINE GRIEZMANN

Known for being the ultimate team player, Antoine Griezmann is able to fulfill all offensive roles, be it front man, attacking midfielder, false 9, or coming from wide positions. He is an excellent teammate, using his experience to improve everyone around him in all situations.

NATIONALITY
French

CURRENT CLUB
Atlético Madrid

DATE OF BIRTH	03/21/1991
POSITION	STRIKER
HEIGHT	5 FT. 9¼ IN.
WEIGHT	161 LB.
PREFERRED FOOT	LEFT

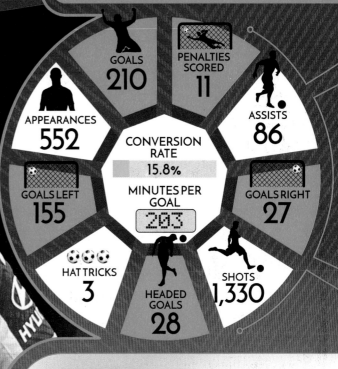

GOALS
210

PENALTIES SCORED
11

ASSISTS
86

APPEARANCES
552

CONVERSION RATE
15.8%

MINUTES PER GOAL
203

GOALS LEFT
155

GOALS RIGHT
27

HAT TRICKS
3

HEADED GOALS
28

SHOTS
1,330

MAJOR CLUB HONORS
⚽ UEFA Champions League: Runner-up 2016
⚽ UEFA Europa League 2018 ⚽ UEFA Super Cup 2018
⚽ Copa del Rey 2021 (Barcelona)

INTERNATIONAL HONORS
⚽ FIFA World Cup: 2018, runner-up 2022
⚽ UEFA European Championship: Runner-up 2016
⚽ UEFA Nations League: 2021

ACTIVITY AREAS

NATIONALITY
Norwegian

CURRENT CLUB
Manchester City

ERLING HAALAND

Erling Haaland has become one of the most exciting forwards in world soccer. He has all the talents: two good feet, blistering pace, good in the air, energy, strength, timing, and the instincts to put the ball in the back of the net.

DATE OF BIRTH	07/21/2000
POSITION	STRIKER
HEIGHT	6 FT. 4¼ IN.
WEIGHT	194 LB.
PREFERRED FOOT	LEFT

GOALS
133

PENALTIES SCORED
19

APPEARANCES
133

ASSISTS
27

CONVERSION RATE
31%

MINUTES PER GOAL
79

GOALS LEFT
95

GOALS RIGHT
22

HAT TRICKS
9

HEADED GOALS
16

SHOTS
430

MAJOR CLUB HONORS
⚽ Premier League: 2023 ⚽ UEFA Champions League: 2023
⚽ DFB-Pokal: 2021 (Borussia Dortmund) ⚽ Austrian
Bundesliga: 2019, 2020 (Red Bull Salzburg) ⚽ FA Cup: 2023
⚽ Austrian Cup: 2019 (Red Bull Salzburg)

INTERNATIONAL HONORS
⚽ None to date

ACTIVITY AREAS

CIRO IMMOBILE

A great team player, Ciro Immobile is a natural finisher who is excellent in the air. His goals tally is even higher, because he refuses to give up lost causes and is willing to chase back to force mistakes out of defenders.

 **NATIONALITY**
Italian

CURRENT CLUB
Lazio

17

DATE OF BIRTH	02/20/1990
POSITION	STRIKER
HEIGHT	6 FT. ¾ IN.
WEIGHT	172 LB.
PREFERRED FOOT	RIGHT

GOALS
224

PENALTIES SCORED
55

APPEARANCES
398

ASSISTS
56

CONVERSION RATE
18.9%

GOALS LEFT
31

MINUTES PER GOAL
132

GOALS RIGHT
169

HAT TRICKS
8

HEADED GOALS
24

SHOTS
1187

MAJOR CLUB HONORS
⚽ Serie A: Runner-up 2023 ⚽ Coppa Italia: 2019

INTERNATIONAL HONORS
✪ UEFA European Championship: 2020
✪ UEFA Nations League: Third place 2023

ACTIVITY AREAS

20

NATIONALITY
Portuguese

CURRENT CLUB
Liverpool

DIOGO JOTA

Most effective as a main striker, Diogo Jota is able to adapt his game to play deeper or as a left winger. He'll wait for defenders to be dragged out of position before running into spaces behind them and shooting powerfully with his right foot.

DATE OF BIRTH	12/04/1996
POSITION	STRIKER
HEIGHT	5 FT. 10 IN.
WEIGHT	150 LB.
PREFERRED FOOT	BOTH

GOALS
59

PENALTIES SCORED
0

APPEARANCES
185

ASSISTS
20

CONVERSION RATE
16.1%

MINUTES PER GOAL
194

GOALS LEFT
19

GOALS RIGHT
30

HAT TRICKS
4

HEADED GOALS
10

SHOTS
367

MAJOR CLUB HONORS
⚽ FA Cup: 2022
⚽ UEFA Champions League: Runner-up 2022

INTERNATIONAL HONORS
⚽ UEFA Nations League: 2019

ACTIVITY AREAS

LUKA JOVIĆ

Luka Jović is a predator in the penalty box. He uses his speed and attacking instincts to find spaces in the penalty area and score goals from close range with deft touches from either foot and occasionally his head.

NATIONALITY
Serbian

CURRENT CLUB
Fiorentina

7

DATE OF BIRTH	12/23/1997
POSITION	STRIKER
HEIGHT	5 FT. 11¼ IN.
WEIGHT	172 LB.
PREFERRED FOOT	RIGHT

GOALS
48

PENALTIES SCORED
1

APPEARANCES
163

ASSISTS
14

CONVERSION RATE
15.6%

MINUTES PER GOAL
162

GOALS LEFT
14

GOALS RIGHT
24

HAT TRICKS
1

HEADED GOALS
10

SHOTS
308

MAJOR CLUB HONORS
- La Liga: 2020, 2022 (Real Madrid)
- UEFA Champions League: 2022 (Real Madrid)
- DFB-Pokal: 2018 (Eintracht Frankfurt)
- UEFA Conference League: Runner-up

INTERNATIONAL HONORS
- None to date

ACTIVITY AREAS

10

NATIONALITY
English

CURRENT CLUB
Tottenham Hotspur

HARRY KANE

Harry Kane has grown into the complete striker. His power in the air, skills with both feet, and superb ball-striking technique make him hard to defend against. What's more, with his defense-splitting passes, he also sets up many goals for his teammates.

DATE OF BIRTH	07/28/1993
POSITION	STRIKER
HEIGHT	6 FT. 2 IN.
WEIGHT	189 LB.
PREFERRED FOOT	RIGHT

GOALS
245

PENALTIES SCORED
37

ASSISTS
56

APPEARANCES
383

CONVERSION RATE
17.8%

MINUTES PER GOAL
1.28

GOALS LEFT
47

GOALS RIGHT
147

HAT TRICKS
10

HEADED GOALS
49

SHOTS
1,373

MAJOR CLUB HONORS
⚽ UEFA Champions League: Runner-up 2019

INTERNATIONAL HONORS
⚽ UEFA European Championship: Runner-up 2020
⚽ UEFA Nations League: Third place 2019

ACTIVITY AREAS

ROBERT LEWANDOWSKI

Robert Lewandowski has consistently ranked as one of the world's best strikers since he made his debut at Borussia Dortmund in 2010. His positioning, technique, power, and finishing saw him net more than 300 goals in the Bundesliga before he made his move to Barcelona in 2022.

NATIONALITY
Polish

CURRENT CLUB
Barcelona

DATE OF BIRTH	08/21/1988
POSITION	STRIKER
HEIGHT	6 FT. ¾ IN.
WEIGHT	179 LB.
PREFERRED FOOT	RIGHT

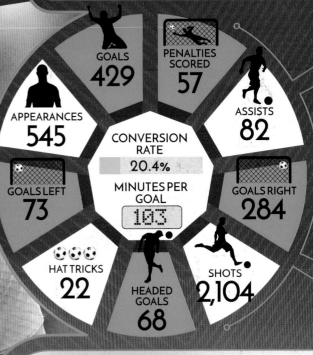

GOALS **429**

PENALTIES SCORED **57**

ASSISTS **82**

APPEARANCES **545**

CONVERSION RATE **20.4%**

MINUTES PER GOAL **103**

GOALS LEFT **73**

GOALS RIGHT **284**

HAT TRICKS **22**

HEADED GOALS **68**

SHOTS **2,104**

MAJOR CLUB HONORS
⚽ La Liga: 2023 ⚽ Bundesliga: 2011, 2012 (all B. Dort.), 2015-22 (8 times, all B. Mun.) ⚽ UEFA Champions League: 2020 (B. Mun) ⚽ FIFA Club World Cup: 2020 (B. Mun.) ⚽ UEFA Super Cup: 2020 (B. Mun.)

INTERNATIONAL HONORS
⚽ None to date

ACTIVITY AREAS

90

NATIONALITY
Belgian

CURRENT CLUB
Inter Milan (on loan)

ROMELU LUKAKU

Romelu Lukaku often uses his size and strength to dispossess defenders before controlling the ball and unleashing a fierce shot or a pass to a well-placed teammate. He is also superb in the air and scores many headers.

DATE OF BIRTH	05/13/1993
POSITION	STRIKER
HEIGHT	6 FT. 3 IN.
WEIGHT	205 LB.
PREFERRED FOOT	LEFT

GOALS
216

PENALTIES SCORED
26

APPEARANCES
449

ASSISTS
64

CONVERSION RATE
19%

MINUTES PER GOAL
153

GOALS LEFT
121

GOALS RIGHT
53

HAT TRICKS
4

HEADED GOALS
39

SHOTS
1,140

MAJOR CLUB HONORS
⚽ Serie A: 2021 ⚽ UEFA Champions League: Runner-up 2023 ⚽ Coppa Italia: 2023 ⚽ FIFA Club World Cup: 2021 (Chelsea) ⚽ UEFA Europa League: Runner-up 2020 (Chelsea) ⚽ Belgian Pro League: 2010 (Anderlecht)

INTERNATIONAL HONORS
⚽ FIFA World Cup: Third place 2018

ACTIVITY AREAS

SADIO MANÉ

Sadio Mané has breathtaking pace and dribbling ability. Although he normally plays on the wing, he can also be dangerous in the middle of the field, because he can leap high to win headers and shoot powerfully with either foot.

NATIONALITY
Senegalese

CURRENT CLUB
TBC

17*

*At Bayern Munich

DATE OF BIRTH	04/10/1992
POSITION	WINGER
HEIGHT	5 FT. 9 IN.
WEIGHT	152 LB.
PREFERRED FOOT	RIGHT

GOALS **149**
PENALTIES SCORED **1**
ASSISTS **51**
APPEARANCES **361**
CONVERSION RATE **18%**
MINUTES PER GOAL **185**
GOALS LEFT **43**
GOALS RIGHT **86**
HAT TRICKS **3**
HEADED GOALS **20**
SHOTS **828**

MAJOR CLUB HONORS

⚽ Bundesliga: 2023 ⚽ Prem. League: 2020 (Liv'pool) ⚽ UEFA Champ. League: 2019 (Liv'pool), runner-up 2018 (Liv'pool), runner-up 2022 (Liv'pool) ⚽ UEFA Super Cup: 2019 (Liv'pool) ⚽ FIFA Club World Cup: 2019 (Liv'pool) ⚽ FA Cup: 2022 (Liv'pool)

INTERNATIONAL HONORS

⚽ CAF Africa Cup of Nations: 2021, runner-up 2019

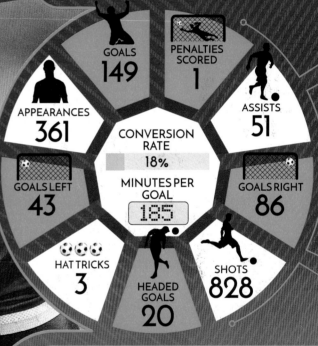

ACTIVITY AREAS

73

7

NATIONALITY
French

CURRENT CLUB
Paris Saint-Germain

KYLIAN MBAPPÉ

A FIFA World Cup winner with France at just 18 and a runner-up four years later, Kylian Mbappé is counted among the best strikers in world soccer today. The pacey finisher is a superb ballplayer who consistently gets on the score sheet and sets up chances for his teammates.

DATE OF BIRTH	12/20/1998
POSITION	STRIKER
HEIGHT	5 FT. 10 IN.
WEIGHT	165 LB.
PREFERRED FOOT	RIGHT

GOALS
204

PENALTIES SCORED
17

ASSISTS
82

APPEARANCES
279

CONVERSION RATE
21.8%

MINUTES PER GOAL
102

GOALS LEFT
42

GOALS RIGHT
154

HAT TRICKS
9

HEADED GOALS
8

SHOTS
936

MAJOR CLUB HONORS
- Ligue 1: 2017 (Monaco), 2018, 2019, 2020, 2022, 2023
- UEFA Champions League: Runner-up 2020
- Coupe de France: 2018, 2020, 2021

INTERNATIONAL HONORS
- FIFA World Cup: 2018, runner-up 2022
- UEFA Nations League: 2021

ACTIVITY AREAS

LIONEL MESSI

The greatest player of his generation, if not the greatest ever, the 2022 World Cup winner is a fine playmaker with a stunning goal-scoring record. He is also a fantastically fast dribbler who can carve out opportunities to shoot with either foot, from any range.

NATIONALITY
Argentinian

CURRENT CLUB
Inter Miami (MLS)

30*

*At Paris Saint-Germain

DATE OF BIRTH	06/24/1987
POSITION	FORWARD
HEIGHT	5 FT. 7 IN.
WEIGHT	159 LB.
PREFERRED FOOT	LEFT

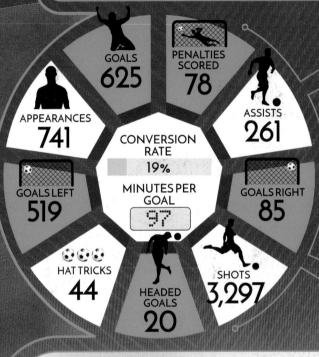

GOALS **625**

PENALTIES SCORED **78**

APPEARANCES **741**

ASSISTS **261**

CONVERSION RATE **19%**

MINUTES PER GOAL **97**

GOALS LEFT **519**

GOALS RIGHT **85**

HAT TRICKS **44**

HEADED GOALS **20**

SHOTS **3,297**

MAJOR CLUB HONORS
⊙ Ligue 1: 2022, 2023 (PSG) ⊙ La Liga: 2005-06, 2009-11, 2013, 2015-16, 2018-19 (all Barca) ⊙ UEFA Champions L.: 2006, 2009, 2011, 2015 (all Barca) ⊙ UEFA Super Cup: 2009, 2011, 2015 (all Barca) ⊙ FIFA Club World Cup: 2009, 2011, 2015 (all Barca)

INTERNATIONAL HONORS
⊙ FIFA World Cup: 2022, runner-up 2014
⊙ Olympic Games: gold medal 2008
⊙ Copa América: 2021, runner-up 2007, 2015, 2016

ACTIVITY AREAS*

19

NATIONALITY
Spanish

CURRENT CLUB
Atlético Madrid

ÁLVARO MORATA

Álvaro Morata is perfectly built for a center striker. Tall, strong, and excellent in the air, he is comfortable with the ball at his feet. Morata is also surprisingly fast and has great tactical and positional awareness.

DATE OF BIRTH	10/23/1992
POSITION	STRIKER
HEIGHT	6 FT. 3¾ IN.
WEIGHT	185 LB.
PREFERRED FOOT	RIGHT

GOALS
132

PENALTIES SCORED
5

APPEARANCES
401

ASSISTS
51

CONVERSION RATE
17.3%

MINUTES PER GOAL
165

GOALS LEFT
32

GOALS RIGHT
67

HAT TRICKS
2

HEADED GOALS
33

SHOTS
765

MAJOR CLUB HONORS

⚽ La Liga: 2012, 2017 (R. Mad.) ⚽ Serie A: 2015, 2016 (Juve.)
⚽ UEFA Champions League: 2014, 2017 (R. Mad.), runner-up 2015 (Juve.) ⚽ UEFA Europa League: 2019 (Chelsea) ⚽ UEFA Super Cup: 2016 (R. Mad.) ⚽ FIFA Club World Cup: 2016 (R. Mad.)

INTERNATIONAL HONORS

⚽ UEFA European U-21 Championship: 2013
⚽ UEFA Nations League: 2023

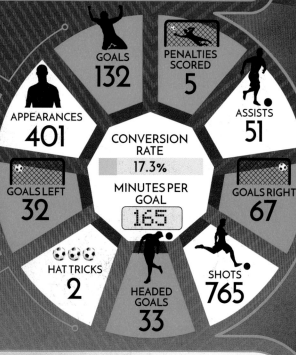

ACTIVITY AREAS

NEYMAR JR.

Neymar is the latest in the long line of great Brazilian strikers. His pace and phenomenal dribbling help him beat defenders in numbers. He strikes fear into the opposition defense with his energetic pace and playmaking skills.

NATIONALITY
Brazilian

CURRENT CLUB
Paris Saint-Germain

10

DATE OF BIRTH	02/05/1992
POSITION	FORWARD
HEIGHT	5 FT. 9 IN.
WEIGHT	150 LB.
PREFERRED FOOT	RIGHT

GOALS
193

PENALTIES SCORED
34

ASSISTS
116

APPEARANCES
316

CONVERSION RATE
18.8%

MINUTES PER GOAL
136

GOALS LEFT
52

GOALS RIGHT
134

HAT TRICKS
8

HEADED GOALS
7

SHOTS
1,027

MAJOR CLUB HONORS
⚽ La Liga: 2015-17 (all Barca) ⚽ Ligue 1: 2018-20, 2022, 2023 ⚽ UEFA Champions League: 2016 (Barca) ⚽ FIFA Club World Cup: 2016 (Barca) ⚽ Copa del Rey: 2015-17 (all Barca) ⚽ Coupe de France: 2018, 2020, 2021

INTERNATIONAL HONORS
⚽ Copa América: Runner-up 2021
⚽ FIFA Confederations Cup: 2013
⚽ Olympic Games: Silver medal 2012, gold medal 2016

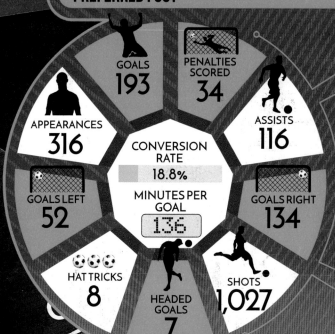

ACTIVITY AREAS

10

NATIONALITY
English

CURRENT CLUB
Manchester United

MARCUS RASHFORD

After a couple of quiet seasons, Marcus Rashford is once again back to his best. He prefers to raid from the left side to be on his stronger right foot, but his pace and heading ability make him just as dangerous in the middle.

DATE OF BIRTH	10/31/1997
POSITION	FORWARD
HEIGHT	5 FT. 10¾ IN.
WEIGHT	154 LB.
PREFERRED FOOT	RIGHT

GOALS
101

PENALTIES SCORED
8

ASSISTS
41

APPEARANCES
304

CONVERSION RATE
14.7%

MINUTES PER GOAL
204

GOALS LEFT
14

GOALS RIGHT
78

HAT TRICKS
1

HEADED GOALS
9

SHOTS
686

MAJOR CLUB HONORS
- ⚽ UEFA Europa League: 2017, runner-up 2021
- ⚽ FA Cup: 2016
- ⚽ English Football League Cup: 2023

INTERNATIONAL HONORS
- ⚽ UEFA European Championship: Runner-up 2021
- ⚽ UEFA Nations League: Third place 2019

ACTIVITY AREAS

MARCO REUS

Marco Reus is an attacker who can lead the front line, play as a second striker, or play out wide. He is an expert finisher, especially with his right foot, and is also fantastic at setting up chances for his teammates.

NATIONALITY
German

CURRENT CLUB
Borussia Dortmund

11

DATE OF BIRTH	05/31/1989
POSITION	FORWARD
HEIGHT	5 FT. 10¾ IN.
WEIGHT	157 LB.
PREFERRED FOOT	RIGHT

GOALS
177

PENALTIES SCORED
17

ASSISTS
103

APPEARANCES
440

CONVERSION RATE
16.7%

MINUTES PER GOAL
193

GOALS LEFT
41

GOALS RIGHT
130

HAT TRICKS
3

HEADED GOALS
6

SHOTS
1,060

MAJOR CLUB HONORS
⚽ Bundesliga: Runner-up 2023
⚽ UEFA Champions League: Runner-up 2013
⚽ DFB-Pokal: 2017, 2021

INTERNATIONAL HONORS
⚽ None to date

ACTIVITY AREAS

NATIONALITY
Egyptian

CURRENT CLUB
Liverpool

MOHAMED SALAH

The two-time African Footballer [Soccer Player] of the Year is a great left-footed attacker who prowls the left wing. Mo Salah has amazing pace with the ability to make angled runs, finding gaps in defenses before scoring spectacular goals.

DATE OF BIRTH	06/15/1992
POSITION	WINGER
HEIGHT	5 FT. 9 IN.
WEIGHT	157 LB.
PREFERRED FOOT	LEFT

GOALS
223

PENALTIES SCORED
25

ASSISTS
97

APPEARANCES
419

CONVERSION RATE
16.9%

MINUTES PER GOAL
149

GOALS LEFT
180

GOALS RIGHT
35

HAT TRICKS
6

HEADED GOALS
8

SHOTS
1,319

MAJOR CLUB HONORS
⚽ Premier League: 2020 ⚽ UEFA Champions League: 2019, runner-up 2018, runner-up 2022 ⚽ UEFA Super Cup: 2019 ⚽ FIFA Club World Cup: 2019 ⚽ FA Cup: 2022

INTERNATIONAL HONORS
⚽ CAF Africa Cup of Nations: Runner-up 2017, runner-up 2021

ACTIVITY AREAS

SON HEUNG-MIN

Son Heung-Min is at his best when he plays behind the main striker. Although excellent with both feet, attacking from the right side is his strength, and he converts a lot of chances that are set up by knockdowns or passes across the box.

NATIONALITY
South Korean

CURRENT CLUB
Tottenham Hotspur

DATE OF BIRTH	07/08/1992
POSITION	WINGER
HEIGHT	6 FT. ½ IN.
WEIGHT	170 LB.
PREFERRED FOOT	BOTH

GOALS
169

PENALTIES SCORED
1

ASSISTS
69

APPEARANCES
474

CONVERSION RATE
16.4%

MINUTES PER GOAL
196

GOALS LEFT
67

GOALS RIGHT
92

HAT TRICKS
5

HEADED GOALS
10

SHOTS
1,029

MAJOR CLUB HONORS
⚽ UEFA Champions League: Runner-up 2019

INTERNATIONAL HONORS
⚽ AFC Asian Cup: Runner-up 2015

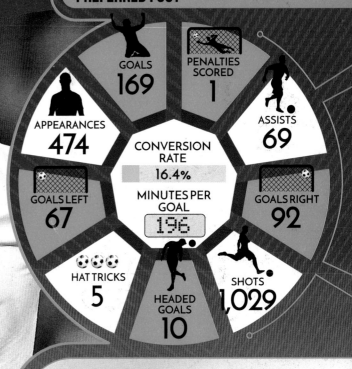

ACTIVITY AREAS

17

NATIONALITY
English

CURRENT CLUB
Chelsea

RAHEEM STERLING

The England international's playing style involves him cutting inside from the left and dribbling past opponents. He also likes to play one-twos with fellow attackers, as well as making runs behind the defensive line to receive a pass that often puts him through on goal.

DATE OF BIRTH	12/08/1994
POSITION	FORWARD
HEIGHT	5 FT. 7 IN.
WEIGHT	152 LB.
PREFERRED FOOT	BOTH

GOALS
142

PENALTIES SCORED
3

ASSISTS
76

APPEARANCES
439

CONVERSION RATE
16.5%

MINUTES PER GOAL
224

GOALS LEFT
36

GOALS RIGHT
95

HAT TRICKS
6

HEADED GOALS
11

SHOTS
859

MAJOR CLUB HONORS
- Premier League: 2018, 2019, 2021, 2022 (all Man. City)
- UEFA Champions League: Runner-up 2021 (Man. City)
- FA Cup: 2019 (Man. City)

INTERNATIONAL HONORS
- UEFA European Championship: Runner-up 2020
- UEFA Europa Nations League: Third place 2019

ACTIVITY AREAS

DUŠAN VLAHOVIĆ

One of world soccer's most exciting rising stars, Dušan Vlahović is very strong and is great in physical battles. He is excellent in the air, winning headers or flicking the ball on, and he almost always converts chances close to goal.

NATIONALITY
Serbian

CURRENT CLUB
Juventus

DATE OF BIRTH	01/28/2000
POSITION	STRIKER
HEIGHT	6 FT. 3¾ IN.
WEIGHT	194 LB.
PREFERRED FOOT	LEFT

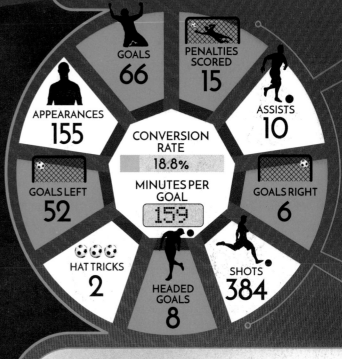

GOALS
66

PENALTIES SCORED
15

ASSISTS
10

APPEARANCES
155

CONVERSION RATE
18.8%

MINUTES PER GOAL
159

GOALS LEFT
52

GOALS RIGHT
6

HAT TRICKS
2

HEADED GOALS
8

SHOTS
384

MAJOR CLUB HONORS
⚽ Serbian SuperLiga: 2017 (Partizan)

INTERNATIONAL HONORS
⚽ None to date

ACTIVITY AREAS

GOALKEEPERS

The goalkeeper is a team's last line of defense and, unlike the other positions, there is no one playing next to them. There is more pressure on goalkeepers than in any other position, because when a keeper makes an error, the chances are that the other team will score. The goalies featured in this section are all great shot stoppers—but some play outside their penalty areas as sweeper keepers; others have made their reputation as penalty savers; and then there are those who are great at catching the ball or punching it clear.

WHAT DO THE STATS MEAN?

CATCHES
This is the number of times the keeper has dealt with an attack—usually a cross—by catching the ball.

PENALTIES FACED/SAVED
This is the number of times a goalie has faced a penalty (excludes shootouts) and how successful he has been at saving it.

CLEAN SHEETS
Any occasion on which the goalie has not let in a goal for the full duration of the game counts as a clean sheet.

PUNCHES
This is a measure of how often the keeper has dealt with a dangerous ball (usually a cross) by punching it clear.

GOALS CONCEDED
This is the number of goals the keeper has conceded in their career in top-division soccer.

SAVES
This shows how many times the goalkeeper has stopped a shot or header that was on target.

Did you
know?

Goalkeepers can, in theory, score goals with their hands. If they throw a ball downfield and it goes directly into the opposition net, the goal will count but, of course, the ball would have to travel about 100 yards.

1

NATIONALITY
Brazilian

CURRENT CLUB
Liverpool

ALISSON

The Brazilian has proved to be a top keeper at Liverpool. Alisson is a superb shot stopper and great at dealing with crosses. Incredibly quick off his line to foil any threat, he can turn defense into attack by finding teammates with long or short passes.

DATE OF BIRTH	10/02/1992
POSITION	GOALKEEPER
HEIGHT	5 FT. 4 IN.
WEIGHT	200 LB.
PREFERRED FOOT	RIGHT

GOALS CONCEDED
251

APPEARANCES
278

PENALTIES SAVED
5

SAVES
707

CLEAN SHEETS
122

PENALTIES FACED
21

PUNCHES
108

CATCHES
123

MAJOR CLUB HONORS
- Premier League: 2020
- UEFA Champions League: 2019, runner-up 2022
- FIFA Club World Cup: 2019
- FA Cup: 2022

INTERNATIONAL HONORS
- Copa América: 2019, runner-up 2021

ACTIVITY AREAS

BONO

Bono (Yassine Bounou) was born in Canada but represents Morocco, the country where he grew up. Very brave and quick to assess dangerous situations, he cuts down angles well, and he's an outstanding shot stopper and also a great communicator.

NATIONALITY
Moroccan

CURRENT CLUB
Sevilla

13

DATE OF BIRTH	05/04/1991
POSITION	GOALKEEPER
HEIGHT	6 FT. 4¾ IN.
WEIGHT	172 LB.
PREFERRED FOOT	RIGHT

GOALS CONCEDED
223

APPEARANCES
192

PENALTIES SAVED
5

CLEAN SHEETS
65

SAVES
562

PENALTIES FACED
35

CATCHES
95

PUNCHES
72

MAJOR CLUB HONORS
⚽ UEFA Europa League: 2020, 2023

INTERNATIONAL HONORS
⚽ None to date

ACTIVITY AREAS

87

1

NATIONALITY
Belgian

CURRENT CLUB
Real Madrid

THIBAUT COURTOIS

Thibaut Courtois uses his height to dominate his penalty area, catching crosses and punching well. An agile shot stopper, he can get down low to make saves, communicates well with his defense, is excellent coming off his line, and passes well.

DATE OF BIRTH	05/11/1992
POSITION	GOALKEEPER
HEIGHT	6 FT. 6¼ IN.
WEIGHT	212 LB.
PREFERRED FOOT	LEFT

GOALS CONCEDED
454

APPEARANCES
492

PENALTIES SAVED
8

CLEAN SHEETS
207

SAVES
1,238

CATCHES
503

PENALTIES FACED
44

PUNCHES
141

MAJOR CLUB HONORS
⚽ La Liga: 2014 (Atlét. Mad.), 2020, 2022, runner-up 2023 ⚽ Prem. League: 2015, 2017 (Chelsea) ⚽ UEFA Champs. League: 2022 ⚽ UEFA Europa L: 2012 (Atlét. Mad.) ⚽ FIFA Club World Cup: 2018 ⚽ UEFA Super Cup: 2012 (Atlét Mad) 2022

INTERNATIONAL HONORS
⚽ FIFA World Cup: Third place 2018

ACTIVITY AREAS

DAVID DE GEA

David De Gea is an effective keeper, although unorthodox at times (he is known for using his legs to make saves). Agile and athletic, he marshals his penalty area well. His catching has improved but he is still happier punching the ball the clear.

NATIONALITY
Spanish

CURRENT CLUB
Manchester United

DATE OF BIRTH	11/07/1990
POSITION	GOALKEEPER
HEIGHT	6 FT. 3½ IN.
WEIGHT	168 LB.
PREFERRED FOOT	RIGHT

GOALS CONCEDED
637

APPEARANCES
568

PENALTIES SAVED
9

CLEAN SHEETS
191

SAVES
1,653

PENALTIES FACED
58

CATCHES
352

PUNCHES
186

MAJOR CLUB HONORS
⚽ Premier League: 2013 ⚽ UEFA Europa League: 2010 (Atlético Mad.), 2017, runner-up 2021 ⚽ UEFA Super Cup: 2010 (Atlético Mad.) ⚽ FA Cup: 2016, runner-up 2023

INTERNATIONAL HONORS
⚽ UEFA Nations League: Runner-up 2021

ACTIVITY AREAS

99

NATIONALITY
Italian

CURRENT CLUB
Paris Saint-Germain

GIANLUIGI DONNARUMMA

The Italian is an amazing talent who made his Serie A debut at just 16 years old, won his first Italian cap at 17, and became a European champion at 22. Mentally strong and composed under pressure, he has everything it takes to become an all-time great.

DATE OF BIRTH	02/25/1999
POSITION	GOALKEEPER
HEIGHT	6 FT. 5 IN.
WEIGHT	198 LB.
PREFERRED FOOT	RIGHT

GOALS CONCEDED
321

APPEARANCES
299

PENALTIES SAVED
10

CLEAN SHEETS
94

SAVES
715

CATCHES
191

PENALTIES FACED
45

PUNCHES
144

MAJOR CLUB HONORS
- ⚽ Ligue 1: 2022, 2023
- ⚽ Supercoppa Italiana: 2016 (AC Milan)

INTERNATIONAL HONORS
- ⚽ UEFA European Championship: 2020
- ⚽ UEFA Nations League: Third place 2021, third place 2023

ACTIVITY AREAS

EDERSON

Due to his range of passing and great ball skills, Ederson is often considered a playmaker goalkeeper and counted as one of the best in the English Premier League. He is a fine shot stopper with a reputation for being a great penalty-kick saver, too.

NATIONALITY
Brazilian

CURRENT CLUB
Manchester City

31

DATE OF BIRTH	08/17/1993
POSITION	GOALKEEPER
HEIGHT	6 FT. 2 IN.
WEIGHT	189 LB.
PREFERRED FOOT	LEFT

GOALS CONCEDED
233

APPEARANCES
290

PENALTIES SAVED
6

CLEAN SHEETS
131

SAVES
529

PENALTIES FACED
34

CATCHES
122

PUNCHES
73

MAJOR CLUB HONORS
⚽ UEFA Champions League: Runner-up 2021, 2023
⚽ Premier League: 2018, 2019, 2021, 2022, 2023
⚽ FA Cup: 2019, 2023

INTERNATIONAL HONORS
⚽ Copa América: 2019, runner-up 2021

ACTIVITY AREAS

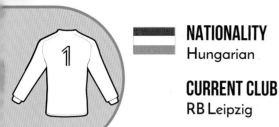

NATIONALITY
Hungarian

CURRENT CLUB
RB Leipzig

PÉTER GULÁCSI

Péter Gulácsi is dedicated to preparing for every soccer situation he faces. He studies approaching forwards to get an instinct for where they are going to shoot, gets into the right position, and then makes difficult saves look easy.

DATE OF BIRTH	05/06/1990
POSITION	GOALKEEPER
HEIGHT	6 FT. 3 IN.
WEIGHT	189 LB.
PREFERRED FOOT	RIGHT

GOALS CONCEDED
320

APPEARANCES
264

PENALTIES SAVED
3

CLEAN SHEETS
78

SAVES
634

PENALTIES FACED
35

CATCHES
154

PUNCHES
67

MAJOR CLUB HONORS
⚽ Austrian Bundesliga: 2014, 2015 (Red Bull Salzburg)
⚽ Austrian Cup: 2014, 2015 (Red Bull Salzburg)
⚽ DFB-Pokal: 2022, 2023

INTERNATIONAL HONORS
⚽ FIFA U-20 World Cup: Third place 2009

ACTIVITY AREAS

SAMIR HANDANOVIĆ

Samir Handanović has awesome positional sense, reaction time, agility, anticipation, and athleticism—a combination that makes him an expert inside the goal. He is also a good communicator and defensive organizer.

NATIONALITY
Slovenian

CURRENT CLUB
Inter Milan

DATE OF BIRTH	07/14/1984
POSITION	GOALKEEPER
HEIGHT	7 FT. 4 IN.
WEIGHT	203 LB.
PREFERRED FOOT	RIGHT

GOALS CONCEDED
696

APPEARANCES
636

PENALTIES SAVED
30

CLEAN SHEETS
222

SAVES
1,840

PENALTIES FACED
94

CATCHES
578

PUNCHES
294

MAJOR CLUB HONORS
- Serie A: 2021
- UEFA Champions League: Runner-up 2023
- Coppa Italia: 2022, 2023

INTERNATIONAL HONORS
- None to date

ACTIVITY AREAS

NATIONALITY
French

CURRENT CLUB
Tottenham Hotspur

HUGO LLORIS

Hugo Lloris is a natural leader, good at organizing his defense. Armed with excellent reflexes, he is brilliant at coming off his line to clear the danger and then distributing the ball quickly, which has earned him the sweeper keeper label.

DATE OF BIRTH	12/26/1986
POSITION	GOALKEEPER
HEIGHT	6 FT. 2 IN.
WEIGHT	181 LB.
PREFERRED FOOT	LEFT

GOALS CONCEDED
740

APPEARANCES
680

PENALTIES SAVED
10

CLEAN SHEETS
231

SAVES
1890

PENALTIES FACED
73

PUNCHES
411

CATCHES
809

MAJOR CLUB HONORS
⚽ UEFA Champions League: Runner-up 2019
⚽ Coupe de France: 2012 (Olympique Lyonnais)

INTERNATIONAL HONORS
⚽ FIFA World Cup: 2018, runner-up 2022
⚽ UEFA Nations League: 2021
⚽ UEFA European Championship: Runner-up 2016

ACTIVITY AREAS

EMILIANO MARTÍNEZ

An immensely athletic goalkeeper, Emiliano Martínez is capable of reaching shots going into the top corner with either hand. His quick feet mean he gets into good positions not only to make saves but also reduce the angle for shots.

NATIONALITY
Argentinian

CURRENT CLUB
Aston Villa

DATE OF BIRTH	09/02/1992
POSITION	GOALKEEPER
HEIGHT	6 FT. 4¾ IN.
WEIGHT	194 LB.
PREFERRED FOOT	RIGHT

GOALS CONCEDED
163

APPEARANCES
139

PENALTIES SAVED
3

CLEAN SHEETS
49

SAVES
416

PENALTIES FACED
20

CATCHES
153

PUNCHES
20

MAJOR CLUB HONORS
⚽ FA Cup: 2020 (Arsenal)

INTERNATIONAL HONORS
⚽ Copa América: 2021
⚽ FIFA World Cup: 2022

ACTIVITY AREAS

NATIONALITY
Senegalese

CURRENT CLUB
Chelsea

ÉDOUARD MENDY

French-born Édouard Mendy chose to play for his mother's birthplace Senegal. He is a great shot stopper who dominates his penalty area, marshals his defense, and deals with aerial threats with supreme confidence.

DATE OF BIRTH	03/01/1992
POSITION	GOALKEEPER
HEIGHT	6 FT. 4¼ IN.
WEIGHT	189 LB.
PREFERRED FOOT	RIGHT

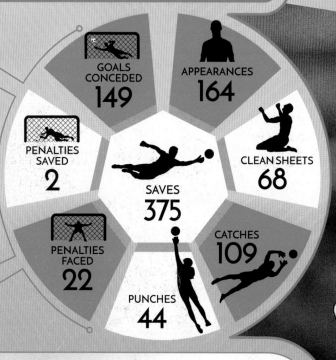

GOALS CONCEDED
149

APPEARANCES
164

CLEAN SHEETS
68

PENALTIES SAVED
2

SAVES
375

PENALTIES FACED
22

PUNCHES
44

CATCHES
109

MAJOR CLUB HONORS
- ⚽ UEFA Champions League: 2021
- ⚽ UEFA Super Cup: 2021
- ⚽ FIFA Club World Cup: 2021

INTERNATIONAL HONORS
- ⚽ CAF Africa Cup of Nations: 2021, runner-up 2019

ACTIVITY AREAS

MANUEL NEUER

Manuel Neuer is famous for being soccer's first sweeper keeper. He is a fine shot stopper who commands his penalty area and marshals the defense well. He is also great with the ball at his feet, allowing defenders to play farther upfield.

NATIONALITY
German

CURRENT CLUB
Bayern Munich

DATE OF BIRTH	03/27/1986
POSITION	GOALKEEPER
HEIGHT	6 FT. 4 IN.
WEIGHT	205 LB.
PREFERRED FOOT	RIGHT

GOALS CONCEDED
520

APPEARANCES
614

PENALTIES SAVED
11

SAVES
1,527

CLEAN SHEETS
270

PENALTIES FACED
43

PUNCHES
270

CATCHES
602

MAJOR CLUB HONORS
⚽ Bundesliga: 2013–2023 (11 times) ⚽ UEFA Champs League: 2013, 2020 ⚽ UEFA Super Cup: 2013, 2020 ⚽ FIFA Club World Cup: 2013, 2020 ⚽ DFB Pokal: 2011 (Schalke 04) 2013-14, 2016, 2019-20

INTERNATIONAL HONORS
⚽ FIFA World Cup: 2014

ACTIVITY AREAS

13

NATIONALITY
Slovenian

CURRENT CLUB
Atlético Madrid

JAN OBLAK

One of the world's most accomplished keepers, Jan Oblak is blessed with quick reflexes and agility, and he's excellent at coming off his line and organizing his defense. His communication skills make him a reliable team vice captain.

DATE OF BIRTH	01/07/1993
POSITION	GOALKEEPER
HEIGHT	6 FT. 2 IN.
WEIGHT	192 LB.
PREFERRED FOOT	RIGHT

GOALS CONCEDED
283

APPEARANCES
379

PENALTIES SAVED
9

SAVES
938

CLEAN SHEETS
184

PENALTIES FACED
41

CATCHES
220

PUNCHES
103

MAJOR CLUB HONORS
⚽ La Liga: 2021
⚽ UEFA Champions League: Runner-up 2016
⚽ UEFA Europa League: 2018
⚽ UEFA Super Cup: 2018

INTERNATIONAL HONORS
⚽ None to date

ACTIVITY AREAS

JORDAN PICKFORD

NATIONALITY
English

CURRENT CLUB
Everton

Playing for Everton, a struggling team in England, Jordan Pickford is kept busy and is an excellent shot stopper. Not the tallest of goalkeepers, he prefers to punch instead of catching the ball, and he is also very good at distributing to teammates.

DATE OF BIRTH	03/07/1994
POSITION	GOALKEEPER
HEIGHT	6 FT. ¾ IN.
WEIGHT	185 LB.
PREFERRED FOOT	LEFT

GOALS CONCEDED
377

APPEARANCES
251

PENALTIES SAVED
5

CLEAN SHEETS
62

SAVES
797

PENALTIES FACED
29

CATCHES
150

PUNCHES
133

MAJOR CLUB HONORS
⚽ None to date

INTERNATIONAL HONORS
⚽ UEFA European Championship: Runner-up 2020
⚽ UEFA Natiom League: Third place 2019

ACTIVITY AREAS

99

22

NICK POPE

Since joining The Magpies, Nick Pope has proved his worth by keeping many clean sheets for his new club. He dominates his penalty area and is excellent at stopping shots, dealing with crosses, and being a sweeper keeper outside the box.

DATE OF BIRTH	94/19/1992
POSITION	GOALKEEPER
HEIGHT	6 FT. 3 IN.
WEIGHT	168 LB.
PREFERRED FOOT	RIGHT

GOALS CONCEDED
201

APPEARANCES
178

PENALTIES SAVED
4

CLEAN SHEETS
60

SAVES
556

PENALTIES FACED
23

CATCHES
203

PUNCHES
75

MAJOR CLUB HONORS
⚽ None to date

INTERNATIONAL HONORS
⚽ None to date

ACTIVITY AREAS

100

KASPER SCHMEICHEL

The son of the legendary keeper Peter Schmeichel, Kasper has many of his father's strengths. He is mentally strong and brilliant in one-on-one situations. He is also superb in the air, commands his penalty area, and is a great ball distributor.

NATIONALITY
Danish

CURRENT CLUB
Nice

DATE OF BIRTH	11/05/1986
POSITION	GOALKEEPER
HEIGHT	6 FT. 2¼ IN.
WEIGHT	194 LB.
PREFERRED FOOT	RIGHT

GOALS CONCEDED
429

APPEARANCES
341

PENALTIES SAVED
11

CLEAN SHEETS
101

SAVES
975

PENALTIES FACED
51

PUNCHES
130

CATCHES
221

MAJOR CLUB HONORS
- Premier League: 2016 (Leicester City)
- FA Cup: 2021 (Leicester City)

INTERNATIONAL HONORS
- None to date

ACTIVITY AREAS

NATIONALITY
Polish

CURRENT CLUB
Juventus

WOJCIECH SZCZĘSNY

Wojciech Szczęsny has grown into one of Europe's top-class keepers. A natural shot stopper with lightning reflexes, he is also great at controlling his penalty area, dealing with crosses, and setting up counterattacks with quick clearances.

DATE OF BIRTH	04/18/1990
POSITION	GOALKEEPER
HEIGHT	6 FT. 4¾ IN.
WEIGHT	198 LB.
PREFERRED FOOT	RIGHT

GOALS CONCEDED
467

APPEARANCES
445

PENALTIES SAVED
15

SAVES
1,177

CLEAN SHEETS
158

PENALTIES FACED
74

PUNCHES
181

CATCHES
365

MAJOR CLUB HONORS
⚽ Serie A: 2018, 2019, 2020 ⚽ FA Cup: 2014, 2015 (Arsenal) ⚽ Coppa Italia: 2018, 2021, runner-up 2020, runner-up 2022

INTERNATIONAL HONORS
⚽ None to date

ACTIVITY AREAS

MARC-ANDRÉ TER STEGEN

NATIONALITY
German

CURRENT CLUB
Barcelona

A great sweeper keeper, Marc-André ter Stegen is simply world class. In addition to his fine goalkeeping qualities, he is exceptional at anticipating opponents who have beaten the offside trap and can rush off his line to meet the danger.

DATE OF BIRTH	04/30/1992
POSITION	GOALKEEPER
HEIGHT	6 FT. 1½ IN.
WEIGHT	187 LB.
PREFERRED FOOT	RIGHT

GOALS CONCEDED
447

APPEARANCES
454

PENALTIES SAVED
7

CLEAN SHEETS
182

SAVES
1,264

PENALTIES FACED
46

CATCHES
456

PUNCHES
192

MAJOR CLUB HONORS

⚽ La Liga: 2015, 2016, 2018, 2019, 2023 ⚽ UEFA Champions League: 2015 ⚽ UEFA Super Cup: 2015 ⚽ FIFA Club World Cup: 2015 ⚽ Copa del Rey: 2015, 2016, 2017, 2018, 2021

INTERNATIONAL HONORS

⚽ FIFA Confederations Cup: 2017

ACTIVITY AREAS

MANAGERS

Head coaches are as different to each other as players who play in different positions. But the majority of the 12 featured in this section have one thing in common: They are all winners, either in their domestic leagues or in continental competitions. Some, such as Laurent Blanc (facing page), were legendary players in their own right and title winners well before they entered management, while others, such as Liverpool boss Jürgen Klopp, did little on the field but have had great success as the brains behind a top side.

WHAT DO THE STATS MEAN?

GAMES MANAGED
This is the number of matches the coach has been in charge of across their career in top-flight soccer.

TEAMS MANAGED
The number of clubs (first teams only) that the coach has managed during their career to date.

WINS
This is the number of games the coach has won, including one leg of a cup tie, even if the tie was lost on aggregate or penalties.

TROPHIES
The trophy list features the head coach's success in domestic top divisions, national and league cups, and international club competitions, except any super cups.

Did you know?

As a manager, Laurent Blanc rarely takes part in training sessions but takes a step back—leaving the technical aspects to his assistants. Instead, he focuses on the players in individual interviews.

CARLO ANCELOTTI

Formerly an international player, Carlo Ancelotti uses different systems depending on the opposition and players available. His favorite formation is 4—4—2, sometimes in a diamond, other times with four midfielders in a line across the field.

NATIONALITY
Italian

CURRENT CLUB
Real Madrid

YEARS AS HEAD COACH: 28

FIRST CLUB: REGGIANA

CLUBS MANAGED	GAMES	LEAGUE TITLES
10	1284	5

WINS	DRAW	LOSSES
756	287	241

CHAMPIONS LEAGUE TROPHIES	EUROPA LEAGUE TROPHIES	OTHER TROPHIES*
4	0	8

MAJOR CLUB HONORS
- ⚽ La Liga: 2022, runner-up 2023
- ⚽ UEFA Champions League: 2003, 2007 (all AC Milan), 2014, 2022
- ⚽ FIFA Club World Cup: 2007 (AC Milan), 2014, 2022
- ⚽ UEFA Super Cup: 1993, 2007 (all AC Milan), 2014, 2022
- ⚽ Serie A: 2004 (AC Milan)
- ⚽ Premier League: 2010 (Chelsea)
- ⚽ Ligue 1: 2013 (Paris St Germain)
- ⚽ Copa del Rey: 2014, 2023
- ⚽ Bundesliga: 2017 (Bayern Munich)

*Excludes Super Cups

LAURENT BLANC

Laurent Blanc has a track record of coaching success in Ligue 1, having been a big-time winner as a player. His coaching policy focuses on being solid in defense and making sure his players are comfortable in possession of the ball.

NATIONALITY
French

CURRENT CLUB
Olympique Lyonnais

YEARS AS HEAD COACH : 16

FIRST CLUB: BORDEAUX

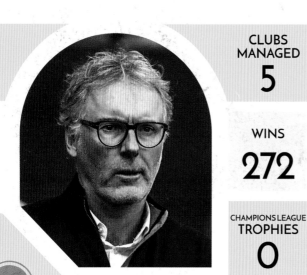

CLUBS MANAGED	GAMES	LEAGUE TITLES
5	447	4

WINS	DRAW	LOSSES
272	87	88

CHAMPIONS LEAGUE TROPHIES	EUROPA LEAGUE TROPHIES	OTHER TROPHIES*
0	0	6

MAJOR CLUB HONORS
- ⚽ Ligue 1: 2009 (Bordeaux), 2014, 2015, 2016 (Paris Saint-Germain)
- ⚽ Coupe de France: 2015, 2016 (Paris Saint-Germain)

*Excludes Super Cups

ANTONIO CONTE

Although Antonio Conte varies his tactics and formations, they are always based on a strong defense, so his teams tend to be great counterattackers. Always animated on the touchline, he instils a great team spirit into his side.

NATIONALITY
Italian

CURRENT CLUB
Free agent

YEARS AS HEAD COACH: 17

FIRST CLUB: AREZZO

CLUBS MANAGED	GAMES	LEAGUE TITLES
9	587	5

WINS	DRAW	LOSSES
342	136	109

CHAMPIONS LEAGUE TROPHIES	EUROPA LEAGUE TROPHIES	OTHER TROPHIES*
0	0	2

MAJOR CLUB HONORS
- ⚽ Serie A: 2012, 2013, 2014 (all Juventus), 2021 (Internazionale)
- ⚽ Premier League: 2017 (Chelsea)
- ⚽ FA Cup: 2018 (Chelsea)
- ⚽ UEFA Europa League: Runner-up 2020 (Inter Milan)

*Excludes Super Cups

UNAI EMERY

Unai Emery has enjoyed great success managing clubs that have a modest budget. His preference is either a 4—2—3—1 formation or 4—4—2, the choice dependent on the attacking skills of the two center midfielders and their ability to retain possession.

NATIONALITY
Spanish

CURRENT CLUB
Aston Villa

YEARS AS HEAD COACH: 19

FIRST CLUB: LORCA DEPORTIVA

CLUBS MANAGED	GAMES	LEAGUE TITLES
9	953	1

WINS	DRAW	LOSSES
508	210	235

CHAMPIONS LEAGUE TROPHIES	EUROPA LEAGUE TROPHIES	OTHER TROPHIES*
0	4	4

MAJOR CLUB HONORS
- ⚽ UEFA Europa League: 2014, 2015, 2016 (all Sevilla), 2021 (Villareal), runner-up 2019 (Arsenal)
- ⚽ Ligue 1: 2018 (Paris Saint-Germain)
- ⚽ Coupe de France: 2017, 2018 (all Paris Saint-Germain)

*Excludes Super Cups

CHRISTOPHE GALTIER

Christophe Galtier builds his teams from the back and is happy to go with either 4–2–3–1 or 4–3–3 formations. He made his reputation as a coach who got teams out of relegation trouble with excellent organization on the field.

NATIONALITY
French

CURRENT CLUB
Paris Saint-Germain

YEARS AS HEAD COACH:	14
FIRST CLUB:	SAINT-ETIENNE

CLUBS MANAGED	GAMES	LEAGUE TITLES
4	606	2

WINS	DRAW	LOSSES
282	155	169

CHAMPIONS LEAGUE TROPHIES	EUROPA LEAGUE TROPHIES	OTHER TROPHIES*
0	0	1

MAJOR CLUB HONORS
- ⚽ Ligue 1: 2021 (Lille), 2023
- ⚽ Coupe de France: Runner-up (Nice)

*Excludes Super Cups

PEP GUARDIOLA

Once a great midfielder himself, Pep Guardiola devised the *tika-taka* passing system at Barcelona (2008–12). Disciplined in possession, without the ball his teams press the opposition into making mistakes and then launch rapid counterattacks.

NATIONALITY
Spanish

CURRENT CLUB
Manchester City

YEARS AS HEAD COACH:	15
FIRST CLUB:	BARCELONA

CLUBS MANAGED	GAMES	LEAGUE TITLES
3	821	11

WINS	DRAW	LOSSES
600	123	98

CHAMPIONS LEAGUE TROPHIES	EUROPA LEAGUE TROPHIES	OTHER TROPHIES*
3	0	13

MAJOR CLUB HONORS
- ⚽ UEFA Champions League: 2009, 2011 (Barcelona), runner-up 2021, 2023
- ⚽ UEFA Super Cup: 2009, 2011 (Barcelona), 2013 (B. Munich)
- ⚽ FIFA Club World Cup: 2009, 2011 (Barcelona), 2013 (B. Munich)
- ⚽ La Liga: 2009, 2010, 2011 (Barcelona)
- ⚽ Bundesliga: 2014, 2015, 2016 (B. Munich)
- ⚽ Premier League: 2018, 2019, 2021, 2022, 2023
- ⚽ FA Cup: 2019, 2023

*Excludes Super Cups

JÜRGEN KLOPP

Jürgen Klopp brings great enthusiasm to the technical area and expects his team to show a similar spirit. His team are strong defensively, try to win back the ball immediately after they lose it, and counterattack at great speed.

NATIONALITY
German

CURRENT CLUB
Liverpool

YEARS AS HEAD COACH: 22

FIRST CLUB: MAINZ 05

CLUBS MANAGED	GAMES	LEAGUE TITLES
3	1022	3

WINS	DRAW	LOSSES
549	245	228

CHAMPIONS LEAGUE TROPHIES	EUROPA LEAGUE TROPHIES	OTHER TROPHIES*
1	0	4

*Excludes Super Cups

MAJOR CLUB HONORS
- ⚽ UEFA Champions League: Runner-up 2013 (B. Dortmund), runner-up 2018, 2019, runner-up 2022
- ⚽ UEFA Super Cup: 2019
- ⚽ FIFA Club World Cup: 2019
- ⚽ Bundesliga: 2011, 2012 (all B. Dortmund)
- ⚽ DFB-Pokal: 2012 (B. Dortmund)
- ⚽ Premier League: 2020
- ⚽ FA Cup: 2022

JULEN LOPETEGUI

Julen Lopetegui likes his teams to be creative in attack and wants his fullbacks to give width, dragging defenders out of position and then filling the gaps they leave behind. He preaches a never-give-up attitude from his teams.

NATIONALITY
Spanish

CURRENT CLUB
Wolverhampton Wanderers

YEARS AS HEAD COACH: 20

FIRST CLUB: RAYO VALLECANO

CLUBS MANAGED	GAMES	LEAGUE TITLES
6	338	0

WINS	DRAW	LOSSES
178	80	80

CHAMPIONS LEAGUE TROPHIES	EUROPA LEAGUE TROPHIES	OTHER TROPHIES*
0	1	0

*Excludes Super Cups

MAJOR CLUB HONORS
- ⚽ UEFA Europa League: 2020 (Sevilla)
- ⚽ UEFA Super Cup: Runner-up 2020 (Sevilla)
- ⚽ UEFA Super Cup: Runner-up 2018 (Real Madrid)

JOSÉ MOURINHO

José Mourinho focuses his team strength on midfield, normally with a player in front of the defense and two or three farther upfield. He expects his defenders to be tactically and technically excellent and tends to pick experienced players.

NATIONALITY
Portuguese

CURRENT CLUB
AS Roma

| YEARS AS HEAD COACH: | 23 |
| FIRST CLUB: | BENFICA |

CLUBS MANAGED	GAMES	LEAGUE TITLES
10	1105	8

WINS	DRAW	LOSSES
688	230	187

CHAMPIONS LEAGUE TROPHIES	EUROPA LEAGUE TROPHIES	OTHER TROPHIES*
2	2	9

*Excludes Super Cups

MAJOR CLUB HONORS
- ⚽ UEFA Champions League: 2004 (Porto), 2010 (Inter Milan)
- ⚽ UEFA Europa League: 2017 (Man Utd), runner-up 2023
- ⚽ UEFA Cup: 2003 (Porto)
- ⚽ Premier League: 2005, 2006, 2015 (all Chelsea)
- ⚽ FA Cup: 2007 (Chelsea)
- ⚽ Serie A: 2009, 2010 (all Inter Milan)
- ⚽ Coppa Italia: 2010 (Inter Milan)
- ⚽ La Liga: 2012 (Real Madrid)
- ⚽ Copa del Rey: 2011 (Real Madrid)
- ⚽ UEFA Europa Conf. League: 2022

THOMAS TUCHEL

Thomas Tuchel has won multiple trophies. He is flexible, changing tactics to suit the players he has available, and is a strong believer in *Gegenpressing*, immediately trying to regain possession instead of dropping into a more defensive mode.

NATIONALITY
German

CURRENT CLUB
Bayern Munich

| YEARS AS HEAD COACH: | 16 |
| FIRST CLUB: | FC AUGSBURG II |

CLUBS MANAGED	GAMES	LEAGUE TITLES
6	529	3

WINS	DRAW	LOSSES
300	108	121

CHAMPIONS LEAGUE TROPHIES	EUROPA LEAGUE TROPHIES	OTHER TROPHIES*
1	0	4

*Excludes Super Cups

MAJOR CLUB HONORS
- ⚽ Bundesliga: 2023
- ⚽ UEFA Champions League: 2021 (Chelsea), runner-up 2020 (PSG)
- ⚽ FIFA World Club Cup: 2021 (Chelsea)
- ⚽ UEFA Super Cup: 2021 (Chelsea)
- ⚽ Ligue 1: 2019, 2020 (all PSG)
- ⚽ Coupe de France: 2020 (PSG)
- ⚽ Trophée des Champions: 2018, 2019 (all PSG)
- ⚽ DfB Pokal: 2017 (Borussia Dortmund)
- ⚽ Coupe de la Ligue: 2020 (PSG)

STEFANO PIOLI

Stefano Pioli is superb at instilling confidence into his players. This is partly because he is flexible with his tactics and focuses more on the management of the individuals, getting the best out of them on the field. He favors a 4–2–3–1 formation.

NATIONALITY
Italian

CURRENT CLUB
AC Milan

| YEARS AS HEAD COACH: | 20 |
| FIRST CLUB: | SALERNITANA |

CLUBS MANAGED	GAMES	LEAGUE TITLES
13	819	1

WINS	DRAW	LOSSES
336	239	244

CHAMPIONS LEAGUE TROPHIES	EUROPA LEAGUE TROPHIES	OTHER TROPHIES*
0	0	0

*Excludes Super Cups

MAJOR CLUB HONORS
- ⚽ Serie A: 2022

DIEGO SIMEONE

Diego Simeone likes to use a formation that is almost a 4–2–2–2 unit, with wide midfielders playing between the two center ones and the strikers. Strong defensively, his teams are great at defending set pieces and are dangerous in attack.

NATIONALITY
Argentinian

CURRENT CLUB
Atlético Madrid

| YEARS AS HEAD COACH: | 17 |
| FIRST CLUB: | RACING CLUB |

CLUBS MANAGED	GAMES	LEAGUE TITLES
6	834	4

WINS	DRAW	LOSSES
465	198	171

CHAMPIONS LEAGUE TROPHIES	EUROPA LEAGUE TROPHIES	OTHER TROPHIES*
0	2	1

MAJOR CLUB HONORS
- ⚽ UEFA Champions League: Runner-up 2014, 2016
- ⚽ UEFA Europa League: 2012, 2018
- ⚽ UEFA Super Cup: 2012, 2018
- ⚽ La Liga: 2014, 2021
- ⚽ Copa del Rey: 2013
- ⚽ Primera División Apertura 2006 (Estudiantes)
- ⚽ Primera División Clausura 2008 (Racing Club)

NOTES